WAFFEN SS

AT WAR

WAFFEN SS

AT WAR

A. J. BARKER

BOOK CLUB ASSOCIATES
LONDON

Oath sworn by the Waffen-SS

*'Ich schwöre Dir, Adolf Hitler, als
Führer und Kanzler des Reiches, Treue
und Tapferkeit. Ich gelobe Dir und
den von Dir bestimmten Vorgesetzten
Gehorsam bis in den Tod, so wahr mir
Gott helfe.'*

('I swear to you, Adolf Hitler,
  Führer and Reich Chancellor,
  Faithfulness and courage. I vow
  to you and to those you set above me
  obedience till death . . .
  So help me God.')

All the photographs in this book were
researched by Andrew Mollo of the
Historical Research Unit.

First published 1982

This edition published 1982 by Book Club
Associates, by arrangement with Ian Allan Ltd

Printed in the United Kingdom by
Ian Allan Printing Ltd

Contents

Introduction

The first divisions of the Waffen-SS were created early in World War 2 from the full-time para-military organisations of the SS already in existence. Hitler's personal bodyguard, the Leibstandarte Adolf Hitler, formed the nucleus of the first of these divisions, and the *SS-Verfügungstruppe* (SS Special Purpose Troops) or SS-VT provided the second division, which was eventually given the name 'Das Reich'.

The Leibstandarte Adolf Hitler had begun its career in 1933 shortly after the Berlin Reichstag was burned down, when Hitler, terrified of plots against his life, ordered the creation of a special bodyguard to protect him. The job of commanding this bodyguard was given to a burly Bavarian, Hitler's old party comrade and chauffeur Josef ('Sepp') Dietrich. Dietrich had set about forming the

unit with his usual energy, selecting 120 men, all over six foot, who formed a triple cordon round Hitler at the Reichskanzlei through which every visitor to the Führer had to pass. Photographs and newsreels of these smart black-clad sentries on guard outside the Reichskanzlei soon became familiar to people all over the world; to many they symbolised the brutal efficiency of the new regime in Germany.

In September 1933, at the Nuremberg Party Rally, Hitler gave his bodyguard, which up to this time had simply been called the 'staff guard', its new name — SS Leibstandarte Adolf Hitler. Two months later, on 9 November, the tenth anniversary of the abortive Munich Putsch, the members of the Leibstandarte were sworn in by a special oath which bound them uncon-

1

ditionally, body and soul, to the person of Adolf Hitler. At the time the new oath escaped the attention of most Germans. The ceremony had been impressive and the tall young men of the Leibstandarte had been excellently turned out, their drill perfect. That was all. What few people appreciated was that Hitler had created a new Praetorian guard as in ancient Rome, a guard which owed its loyalty not to the state but to the ruler of that state.

Dietrich himself had little knowledge of modern warfare — although he had served as a sergeant in the old Bavarian Army from 1911 to 1918. He looked like a butcher (which is what he had once been) but he was without doubt tough, brave and possessed moral courage — qualities which made him popular with his men. He was, however, no leader. As one of his corps commanders, General Willi Bittrich, said of him to the author: 'I once spent an hour and a half with the aid of my map trying to explain a situation to Sepp Dietrich. But it was quite hopeless; he just could not grasp the facts'. Göring is reputed to have said of him: 'He had, at the most, only the ability to command a division'; and von Rundstedt bitingly summed him up as 'decent but stupid'. Nevertheless Sepp Dietrich rose to the rank of SS-Oberstgruppenführer.

The SS-VT, the second forerunner formation of the Waffen-SS, was formed in March 1935 from battalions of the *SS Politische Bereitschaften* (Political Readiness Squads) — full-time, armed units of men trained for 'heavy police' tasks and internal security duties. Like the Leibstandarte the SS-VT was transformed into a military force. Commanding the SS-VT at this time was the man who was to prove to be the ablest military commander in the SS — Paul Hausser. Hausser, who was 59 in 1939, had retired from the old Imperial Army with the rank of lieutenant-general. He was an officer of the old school, experienced in staff work, and having joined Himmler's political police force in 1933, he had set up a training school and made a good job of it. Like Dietrich, Hausser was also to reach the rank of SS-Oberstgruppenführer.

Following the creation of the first two Waffen-SS divisions, elements of the *SS Totenkopfverbände* (SS Death's Head Regiments) or SS-TV were amalgamated and expanded to form a third division. German policemen provided a fourth. Then came others based on units of the Death's Head Regiments which had not been incorporated in the third division. Men of German blood resident outside the Reich — the so-called Volksdeutsche — also joined the Waffen-SS in considerable numbers and whole divisions, like the Prinz Eugen, were built up around them. Then, following the German conquest of western and northern Europe, volunteers were enlisted from the so-called 'Nordic' countries and after some time these were grouped into 'Germanic' divisions of the Waffen-SS. 'Non-Germanic' western Europeans, such as French, Walloon and Italian volunteers, were eventually also

1
Men of the Leibstandarte undergoing basic training on the drill square, 1936.

2
The Leibstandarte on a route march during training in Jüterbog, c1934.

grouped into divisions.* Finally when the grandiose racial requirements for membership of the SS had to be sacrificed to the demands of war, whole SS divisions were formed from what the Nazis believed to be 'inferior' races like the Russians. At the end of the war in 1945 no less than 38 Waffen-SS divisions appeared in the German Order of Battle although 14 of these were only of regimental strength or less, and some of the others had been decimated.

By 1942 all the Waffen-SS divisions then in existence had been motorised, and as each had an SS-Panzer regiment, they were panzer divisions in all but name. Before the end of 1942, however, they were redesignated 'panzergrenadier' divisions, and their infantry regiments designated panzergrenadier regiments.

The basic organisation of a Waffen-SS division based on that of the Leibstandarte is given in Appendix 3. In reading this it must be remembered that the fortunes of war, the acquisition of foreign volunteers and other factors led to considerable structural changes in individual divisions, and the divisional orders of battle changed continually. Moreover many units were redesignated during their comparatively short lives, especially when the parent divisions were first partially, and then fully motorised. One could find the self-same regiment at first designated as a *Schützen-Regiment* (rifle regiment), then an *Infanterie-Regiment* (infantry regiment), next a *Grenadier-Regiment* (grenadier regiment) and finally a *Panzergrenadier-Regiment* (armoured grenadier regiment). Another factor was the often very slender continuity, for new elements would be created in the West, while remnants of the old ones were still in the East. Other units were transferred from one division to another and therefore redesignated, whereas others were reclassified en masse throughout the Wehrmacht and Waffen-SS (eg in the late summer of 1944, all SS-Wirtschafts Bataillone were renamed SS-Verwaltungs

Abteilungen). Such changes were numerous, frequent and often involved but they do not affect the story of the Waffen-SS 'at war' and so there is little purpose in trying to disentangle these changes in the story that follows.

When the SS was created Himmler decided that its members should all be volunteers, aged between 17 and 22, at least 5ft 11in tall and of the highest physical fitness. Every man had to be of well-proportioned build. Himmler used to boast that 'until 1936 we did not accept a man in the Leibstandarte . . . if he had even one filled tooth. We were able to assemble the most magnificent manhood in that early Waffen-SS'. Moreover recruits had to look 'truly Nordic' and their Aryan pedigree had to be spotless. From the end of 1935 every SS man had to be able to produce a record of his ancestry— for other ranks back to 1800, for officers back to 1750. And if a trace of Jewish or other 'undesirable' blood was detected, the man was refused entry or, if it came to light later, expelled from the SS. 'Sepp' Dietrich commented in disgust: 'Some 40 good specimens at least are kept from

*There was even a tiny British contingent — the SS Legion of St George — consisting of a handful of British renegade prisoners-of-war, their SS uniforms bearing Union Jack shoulder flashes. This British SS Legion did not go into action although it was sent up to the Eastern Front when the Russians were within 50 miles of Berlin. According to reports when they reported to SS Division HQ the divisional commander ordered them to go back to Berlin. 'We have a war on our hands', he is reputed to have said. 'We need proper soldiers, not amateurs.'

3
Hitler congratulates newly commissioned SS officers in the Mosaic Hall of the Reichskanzlei, on his 50th birthday, 1938. Himmler, the Reichsführer-SS, is on Hitler's left.

4
An SS-Totenkopf battalion on the march, 1936.

joining the Leibstandarte every year, due to doubt concerning ancestry'. (As a corollary to this, any woman wishing to marry an SS man had to submit her ancestry for examination, together with a photograph of herself in a bathing costume.)

Prior to the outbreak of war membership of the armed SS was voluntary and, even when the exigencies of war forced it to accept numbers of conscripts, this aspect remained important. As an SS instruction put it: 'A decision to join the Führer's military force is equally nothing less than the expression of a voluntary determination to continue the present political struggle upon another level'. From 1935, membership of the Leibstandarte and SS-VT counted as military service, but its terms were hard — a minimum of four years for enlisted men, 12 for NCOs and 25 for officers. Rates of pay, from August 1938, corresponded to those of the Wehrmacht. Before 1939, a member of the SS-VT could always obtain his release from its ranks if he were sufficiently determined to do so (in 1937, for example, 84 men left), but the war put an end to this.

Although considerable restrictions were placed upon recruitment to the Waffen-SS — for example, before the war it was not allowed to advertise in the press — the desire of many young Germans to become members of an ideological and military elite, coupled with Hitler's endeavours to keep his guard up to strength, ensured that SS units generally had few manpower problems. However, war inevitably took its toll both in quality and quantity, and by 1943 the Waffen-SS had been forced to lower its standards. Ethnic Germans from Hungary, Slovakia and Romania, some of who were in their 50s, were even to be found within its ranks. Indeed the last draft received by the Leibstandarte consisted of an assorted collection of personnel from the Luftwaffe, the Navy and the factories, a proportion of whom were above active-service age.

Following the outbreak of war, service in the Waffen-SS remained voluntary but, in fact, from 1943 onwards, members of the Hitler Youth as well as others were subjected to a certain degree of pressure to join. Germany itself was divided into SS 'districts'

5

10

(*SS-Oberabschnitte*) each of which had a recruiting centre, which carried the same name as the district and the Roman numeral of the military district (*Wehrkreis*) and was usually located at the latter's HQ town. Some of the recruiting centres also maintained branch offices outside Germany for the recruitment of racial Germans (*Volksdeutsche*). However, in January 1945, the recruiting centres for the Waffen-SS in Germany were combined with those of the army, and the resulting centres (*Ergänzungsstellen des Heeres und der Waffen-SS*) in each military district had branch offices in all major German towns.

Outside Germany, the method of recruiting depended on the particular country in question. In those with a high degree of collaboration and where Nazi or Quisling parties had developed, the local collaborators were used. Otherwise, the German-controlled governments dealt with the matter, or the German authorities had an agreement with the respective government. At first, recruiting outside Germany was carried on by a number of recruiting commands (*Ersatzkom-mandos der Waffen-SS*), which were to be found in the principal towns of the occupied countries. Later these were reorganised as recruiting inspectorates (*Ersatzinspektionen der Waffen-SS*) which controlled a number of recruiting commands. These commands were divided into enlistment centres (*Werbestellen*).*

In the Waffen-SS great emphasis was placed on 'hardness' and training was extremely rigorous, comparable perhaps with that at the British Brigade of Guards depot or with the basic training to which US Marine Corps personnel were subjected before World War 2. The SS soldier was expected to be 'supple, adaptable, of an athletic bearing, and capable of more than average endurance on the march and in

*The basic recruiting booklet used by the Waffen-SS was called *Dich ruft die SS*, which was translated into various other languages (eg the Dutch version was called *Een Loopbaan voor U — SS*). The press, both in Germany and the occupied countries, was full of propaganda reports from the SS war correspondents which glorified the achievements of the Waffen-SS front-line soldiers and urged readers to join.

5
The SS-VT on the march,
26 February 1933.

6
The Nazi leader in Danzig, Albert Forster, reviewing the local SS Heimwehr (Home Guard) on 18 August 1939. Notice that he is out of step with the Heimwehr commander, Joachim Goetze.

7

8

combat'. There was of course nothing new in training a soldier to have these qualities but the concept of hardness was extended to the ideological side, and the SS man was expected to be insensible, merciless and savage to his opponents. According to Himmler:

'For the SS man there is one absolute principle; he must be honest, decent, loyal and friendly to persons of our own blood, and to no one else . . . I am totally indifferent to what happens to the Russians or the Czechs. If, for instance, an anti-tank ditch has to be dug and 10,000 Russian women die of exhaustion digging it, my only interest is whether the ditch is completed for the benefit of Germany. We will never be savage or heartless where we do not have to be; that is clear. Germans, after all, are the only people in the world who know how to treat animals properly; so we shall know how to treat these human animals properly. But it is a crime against our own blood to worry too much about them and to try to instil ideals into them; we shall only be creating greater

7
SS men deployed in the Sudeten village of Liebenstein in September 1938.

8
Young SS recruits learn to use the compass, 1942.

9
Waffen-SS troops on a route march, 1941-2.

9

10
SS-Gruppenführer Gottlob Berger, Waffen-SS recruiter-in-chief.

11
Himmler visits SS units in the Ukraine late summer 1941.

difficulties for our sons and grandsons. If someone comes to me and says: "I cannot dig this anti-tank ditch with these women and children. It is inhuman; they will die doing it" — my reply must be: "You are a murderer of people of our own blood; if the anti-tank ditch is not dug, German soldiers will die, sons of German mothers. They are our blood." This is what I have tried to instil into the SS and I believe I have done so; it is one of the most sacred laws of the future — all our care and all our duty is to our people and to our blood; that is what we must care for, think about, work for, fight for — that and nothing else. We can be completely indifferent to everything else. This is the attitude which I wish the SS to adopt to the problem of all foreign non-Germanic peoples and above all to the Russians. Everything

else is verbiage, a betrayal of our own people and hindrance to the rapid conclusion of this war.'

The foregoing passage is from Himmler's famous speech in Posnan on 4 October 1945, and serves to explain the attitude of mind instilled in the Waffen-SS troops who committed appalling atrocities during the course of the war.

On the military side training in 'hardness' meant iron discipline and, sometimes, humiliation. According to one ex-Waffen-SS man:

'There was a special method of humiliating a man. If anyone, while filling cartridges into a charger, let a cartridge fall to the ground, he had to pick it up with his teeth. I made up my mind that I would not do that. They can do what they like with me, I said, but I will not pick up a cartridge with my teeth; I shall use my hand. Naturally I took care not to let the situation arise and determined to do everything I could not to let a cartridge fall to the ground. One day of course it happened. On these occasions no one gives an order; the NCO simply turns down his thumb and the man concerned knows what he has to do. In my case of course he turned down his thumb, and I bent down and picked the cartridge up with my hand. He rushed at me like a wild animal, stuck his face close up to mine so that there was hardly an inch between his nose and mine and bellowed whatever came into his head. Of course I could not understand a word because he was bellowing so loud that he was choking. Eventually I gathered that he was yelling: "Have you forgotten what to do?" When he had finished bellowing he handed me over to the deputy section commander who made me do a 10-minute "showpiece". That's a long time when you're at the double all the time. And it's embroidered with all the usual well-known "additions". After such a chasing your shirt is wringing wet. Then the deputy commander handed me back to the commander himself. His first order was: "Chuck that cartridge away." I was not ready for that, I was practically all in. I threw the cartridge away; it fell some six feet away from me — and he turned his thumb down once more. I hesitated for a second. Seeing this he came up to me. I was almost at the stage of picking it up with my teeth. But then, I just wasn't thinking, and I don't know why, again I picked up the cartridge with my hand. That was it! He went scarlet, bellowed out

14

something unintelligible, handed the section over to his deputy and took me on himself. He began with 50 "knee-bends" with rifle held out at arm's length. I had to count out loud. I was fairly fit and I had got used to anything here, but to be asked to do 50 knee-bends with your rifle held out in front of you, following 10 minutes "showpiece" which has left you little better than a jelly, that's a tall order. I'm not saying that it's physically impossible. The only question is whether one is ready for it mentally. And this was what happened. After 20 knee-bends I stopped counting. I just couldn't go on. I did one more knee-bend and then I lowered my rifle and stood up. I can't say that I thought this out; I just knew that I was all in. I heard him bellowing all over again but that left me cold because suddenly I could control myself no longer. I felt I had to weep although I knew that it was neither manly nor soldierly. I couldn't answer his questions because I was so shaken with sobbing that I couldn't speak. I was not in a rage and I was not in pain. I had just had enough. When he saw that he bellowed: "Look at this!" and then: "Mollycoddle! Mother's little darling! Crybaby! Who's ever heard of an SS man blubbering! All our dead will turn in their graves! Is this what we're trying to take to war, etc, etc." Then "assembly" was blown and the training period ended. He ordered me to clean out all the first floor latrines for a week and then report to him so that he could inspect them. And straightaway he ordered: "Chuck this cartridge away." I did so and then without even waiting or looking to see whether he had turned his thumb down I picked it up with my teeth . . .'

Another example of SS inhumanity is to be found in a letter from another SS man, written in 1943:
'Our Commander's a crazy bastard! We could hardly be away for a moment without acts of sabotage occurring. There were guerilla attacks too. When this happened the best our Commander could think up was to take 10 or 20 men from the unsuspecting population in the places where these things happened and have them hanged. Every time he ordered me: "Get a gallows ready." You can imagine how shattered I was when given this order for the first time. I said to him: "Sturmbannführer, I ask you to release me from this order." He merely said: "Milksop! And you want to be an SS man!" I had to carry out the order. The pencil was quivering

in my hand as I sat at my table and thought how to construct a gallows. I never drew one out; I simply went down to the carpenter's shop and asked the people there to help me. I didn't have to ask twice — they had got a gallows ready quick enough and so I could report: "Sturmbannführer, order carried out." I was not present at the execution but from then on I always had a picture in my mind of the gallows which I had had made — with a man hanging on it. Of course it amused the Commander to torment me and whenever there was an execution — that was fairly often — would come the same sarcastic order: "Sturmann X, you are the gallows expert. Get a two-, three- or four-man gallows ready." Each time I would go down to the carpenter's shop and have the gallows made. Everybody used to get leave except me. The Commander was of course afraid that I wouldn't come back. He would always say to me: "You are still under stoppage of leave." Two months ago, however, he drove over a mine and was blown up. So I got a new Commander and he let me go home on leave. But I shall not go back, because they've turned me into a hangman's assistant. All I want is to forget the picture which I see day and night — a gallows with two, three, four or five men hanging on it. What have they done to me! I wanted to be an engineer and my Commander calls me a "gallows expert". I can't go back no matter what happens; I won't go back to those criminals.'

These stories of the 'gallows expert' and the recruit who had to pick up a cartridge with his teeth emphasise that ferocious 'hardness' was applied only to those Waffen-SS men who for some reason or other did not altogether 'belong' — in other words to recruits and to those who, rightly or wrongly, were thought to be independent spirits or weaklings. In this the Waffen-SS was little different from the Wehrmacht, where extra drill was given to those who 'failed to comply' or who fell foul of an NCO. On the other hand for the fully committed SS soldier — the man who actually did 'belong' — the exaggerated harshness of the hardness training were mitigated by the concept known as 'cameraderie'. And it is this spirit of cameraderie which today motivates the veterans of the Waffen-SS in their campaign to win the 'full combatant' status denied to them by the Nuremberg Tribunals ruling that the SS was a criminal organisation.

1
Poland 1939

The first units of the Waffen-SS were blooded in Poland, and the Leibstandarte which fought as an armoured infantry division suffered higher casualties than any of the other regular Wehrmacht units in the corps to which it was attached.

Altogether some 18,000 Waffen-SS from the Leibstandarte, Verfügungstruppe and Totenkopf units participated in the campaign. Most of them had concentrated in East Prussia during August, moving by sea. At the beginning of August 1938, before the 25th anniversary of the battle of Tannenberg, few Germans thought that they would be going to war over Poland and most of the Waffen-SS believed they were involved in just another series of army manoeuvres. The Leibstandarte constituted part of General Walther von Reichenau's Tenth Army and the bulk of the Verfügungstruppe were concentrated in a mixed panzer regiment under the command of Lt-Gen Werner von Kempf. Of this division's three regiments one was SS — the SS-Standarte Deutschland — but the armoured regiment, the 7th Panzer, was a regular Wehrmacht formation and, as the SS lacked trained senior officers, most of von Kempf's staff were Wehrmacht men.

On 30 August Hitler decided that war was inevitable and during the following night SS units staged 'incidents' along the German-Polish border, of which the most notorious was an alleged raid on the radio station at Gleiwitz (now Glivice) in Silesia. Before sunrise on the next morning, 1 September, under cover of a pre-dawn air bombardment, 60 German divisions under the overall command of General Walther von Brauchitsch — nine of them armoured — invaded Poland from the north, west and south. 'The light is very poor,' wrote one SS soldier. '... Today we shall be at war with Poland unless the Poles see sense. Tomorrow I shall be a complete soldier ... now I have time for thinking about only one thing: Germany ...'

Hitler's aim was to fight a short war that would be over before the British or French armies could get into action — over, in fact, before the Western powers could even make up their minds to fight. To fulfil this aim the German plan called for a double pincer envelopment by two groups of armies which would grip the six Polish armies deployed in a defensive cordon along the line of the Vistula River. The Third and Fourth Armies

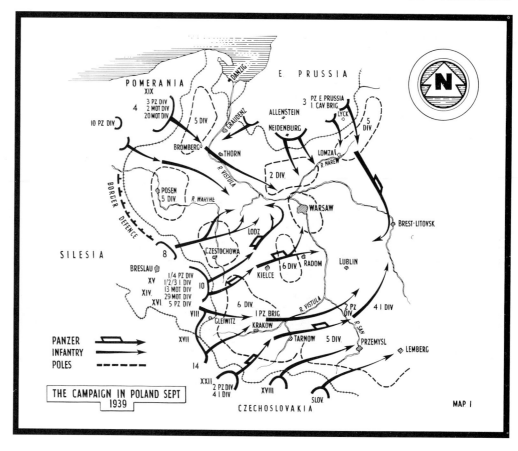

PANZER
INFANTRY
POLES

THE CAMPAIGN IN POLAND SEPT 1939

MAP 1

from General Fedor von Bock's Army Group North would converge on the Polish corridor from both sides — ie from East Prussia and Pomerania — and when they had made contact in the corridor they would advance westwards towards Warsaw. Meantime General Gerd von Runstedt's Army Group South was to sweep eastwards and north-eastwards from Silesia and Slovakia. To support the offensive some 1,600 Luftwaffe aircraft would bomb all the principal cities, destroy the Polish airfields and railway centres, strafe the main highways to dislocate traffic and give close support to the ground troops.

The Polish Army, 32 divisions strong, was inferior to the Wehrmacht qualitatively as well as quantitatively. The German armies were numerically twice as strong in infantry, had four times as many guns, and for every tank fielded by the Poles, the Germans had eight. Furthermore the Polish armour comprised 8ton mini-tanks, and the Poles' supply system was wholly dependent on horsedrawn transport.

The Poles might have been able to counter the German invasion successfully, if they had given ground, fallen back and fought a delaying action until the Western powers could bring their forces to bear. But such a strategy would have meant abandoning the highly populated region in the western half of the country where Poland's industry was concentrated. So the Polish General Staff elected to defend all its frontiers and the fact that this meant spreading the troops thinly on the ground automatically carried the seeds of eventual defeat. But like the SS men the Poles did not really believe there would be a war and, even if there was, that it would follow the pattern of previous conflicts starting with border skirmishes which would gradually evolve into full scale battles. Consequently there would be time for Britain and France to come to their aid.

In the event the Polish air force was virtually destroyed by the Luftwaffe on the morning of 1 September and by the third day it had ceased to exist. By then also there was no communication between the Polish GHQ and its armies in the field. There were two million German sympathisers in the Polish population, and so fifth column and intelligence activities were well organised. Working on information supplied by spies the Luftwaffe bombed the location of Polish headquarters continuously. By 5 September the first phase of the German campaign — the breakthrough on the borders — was over; two armies of von Bock's Army Group North had cut the corridor and had begun turning south-east. Two days later the

12
Poland, September 1939. SS artillery opens fire on the Danzig Post Office. (BA)

12

19

13

Germans were within 25 miles of Warsaw. The Poles fought gallantly but their cavalry was no match for tanks.

At the start of the campaign the SS Germania Regiment was deployed on the right flank of the Fourteenth Army. When the invasion began the Germania advanced through the industrial region towards Lwow. The Poles in this area put up a stiff resistance and the SS men suffered heavy casualties. Losses among the officers were especially high — the regimental commander himself being killed in the course of an action in which the SS subsequently claimed they had received insufficient support from the Wehrmacht divisional units. 'What we needed,' said the new regimental commander, 'was our own SS division. We were given a task which it was unreasonable to expect us to fulfil without adequate support — which wasn't forthcoming from the Wehrmacht.'

With or without Wehrmacht support the young volunteer SS troops fought with a fanatical fury that matched that of the Poles. With the fluency which intensive training brings, they moved steadily forward in section and platoon formations, in accordance with the lessons of fire and movement they had learned on the barrack square and on manoeuvres all over Germany. Generally these tactics proved irresistible and the Poles were usually swept from their positions. But sometimes the Poles struck back, counter-attacking with the bayonet. '... They came into the attack in long lines, not quite shoulder to shoulder, but very close together. They had a battle cry ... and we could also hear the officers shouting ...

14

somebody said they were shouting "Forward, forward"...'

Von Kempf's division formed part of von Bock's Third Army under General Georg von Küchler. Advancing southwards from East Prussia the division was stopped when it ran into Polish entrenched positions near Mlawa. Following a fierce battle in which, yet again, the SS units suffered heavy casualties, von Kempf's division was ordered to pull back. General Heinz Guderian's tanks had effected a spectacular breakthrough on von Bock's left flank, and von Kempf's division was sent after them. The Poles fought with desperate gallantry but now that their defensive line had been penetrated they had no hope of stopping the armour. Consequently the battles which took place in this second phase of the invasion were very much a one-sided affair and the SS men's blooding was that much less intense. Meantime Guderian's panzers had crossed the Narew River, heading for Brest; below Brest, with von Kempf's SS regiments streaming behind them they had crossed the Bug and were driving hard for Deblin, a famous old fortress on the Vistula 60 miles south-east of Warsaw. Many minor engagements were fought out on this advance and German casualties began to mount. The broken country here was ideal for defence and the small groups of Poles, many armed with machine guns, set up defensive positions blocking the roads. Guderian's tanks merely drove around them, and the task of winkling out the defenders fell to the Wehrmacht infantry and SS troops following up. The SS operations were fiercely contested and the Polish riflemen, many of whom were skilled marksmen, inflicted most of the casualties sustained at this time. Well camouflaged and often hidden in positions set high in trees the Poles would pick off individual Germans and shoot up motorcycle despatch riders and staff cars. The SS responded with prophylactic fire — blasting suspected trees and bushes on their line of advance and bombarding them with rifle grenades.

'The Poles are devilishly cunning... Yesterday we had to clear a group of them out of a maize field. We thought they were a party of stragglers and that turfing them out would be a quick and easy operation... But they had dug themselves in and had camouflaged their positions with plants over the top so that it was difficult to spot them. We... had to stalk them like characters from a Karl May Wild West novel. When we found a dug-out we blew it up with bundles of grenades... it took us hours...'

While von Küchler's Third Army was pressing down on Brest, and Guderian's panzers were driving towards Deblin, von Rundstedt's Fourteenth Army — to which the SS Standarte 2 'Germania' Regiment was attached — was streaming in a north-easterly direction past Cracow. And in the centre General Walther von Reichenau's Tenth Army with the majority of the German tank divisions was heading for the Vistula below Warsaw, where he would join hands with Guderian's force. The inner ring of the double envelopment was closing on the Vistula line, the outer ring on the Bug. The principal Polish resistance now centred around the Warsaw-Modlin area and further west around Kutno and Lodz.

On 17 September the 23rd Panzer Regiment attempted to take Lodz. But the attack failed because the Poles had developed a new anti-tank gunnery technique. Aiming at the same spot on a tank they would fire two rounds in quick succession. Against the lightly armoured Mark I and Mark II German tanks one round from the Polish anti-tank guns would be sufficient even at quite long ranges. And at close range the double punch could knock out even the more heavily armoured Mark IIIs and Mark IVs. Having lost a sizeable proportion of his vehicles the commander of the 23rd Panzer Regiment stopped the attack and pulled back. He had not even managed to clear the little town of Pabianice on the Lodz road. 'But this,' he said, 'was a job for the infantry' and two companies of the SS Leibstandarte were ordered up. As the tanks withdrew — still under heavy fire — the SS men shook out into open order and started their advance. Wehrmacht artillery forward observation officers and their own battalion mortar platoon commander moved with them, directing fire on to Polish centres of resistance. The first objective was Pabianice and for a time it looked as if the SS would

13
An SS armoured car in the fighting in Danzig, September 1939.

14
A squad of SS Einsatzkommandos (assault troops) receives its orders, Poland 1939.

15
SS-Standartenführer Heinz Harmel (who later commanded the Frundsberg Division at Arnhem) seen here with Himmler, Paul Hausser and SS-Obergruppenführer Karl Wolff in Poland, 1939.

attain it without too much trouble. Sheer determination carried them through the outer Polish defences into the centre of the town where all hell was let loose. Time and again the Poles counter-attacked with both infantry and cavalry, charging down the open streets and directing the fire of every available weapon, including anti-tank guns, at the SS troops. Other Poles managed to find their way around the German flank and get in behind the attackers, sniping and hurling grenades. The Poles lost a lot of men in these attacks, but so too did the Leibstandarte and the only available reinforcements were the unit's headquarter personnel — mainly cooks and drivers. These were thrown into the fray, and eventually the intensity of the fighting diminished as the Polish effort faded. A point of exhaustion had been reached and the battle was broken off for a few hours while both sides prepared for the next round. This came in the afternoon when the Poles launched yet another counter-attack. '... They stormed over the bodies of their fallen comrades. They did not come forward with their heads down like men in heavy rain — and most attacking infantry come on like that — but they advanced with their heads held high like swimmers breasting the waves. They did not falter . . .'

Brave as they were, there was a limit to the Poles' endurance. As they advanced towards the positions taken up by the SS the lines of Polish infantry were mowed down by a hurricane of shells and bullets. With the failure of this assault the heart went out of the defenders of Pabianice and the Poles started to surrender. The situation which had looked critical for the two Leibstandarte companies in the morning had been restored, although by the end of the day the SS troops were so exhausted and disorganised that the advance on Lodz could not be resumed until they had rested.

By now however von Reichenau's tanks had opened a gap in the Polish defensive line and were all set to roar up the main road to Warsaw. But motorised infantry were needed for the advance, and so the Leibstandarte was pulled out of the fighting for Lodz and sent off to join the Tenth Army's 4th Panzer Division whose forward units were already in Ochota, a Warsaw suburb.

The 1st Battalion of the Leibstandarte was ordered to capture the town of Oltarzev on the Warsaw road while the 2nd and 3rd Battalions were given the important road and rail junction of Blonie — also on the Warsaw road — as their objective. All three battalions encountered fierce resistance as the Poles were striving to keep the road open for their supply columns. Artillery was brought up to support the SS, and the confused mass of Polish troops, transport and refugees that had been stopped by the German roadblocks, was subjected to an all night bombardment. When dawn broke an appalling sight was revealed — heaps of dead and dying men, horses and cattle lay inextricably mixed in the ditches and along the road.

From 10 September and for the following two days the Poles tried to break through the German block near Blonie, without success. A regiment of the 4th Panzer Division supported by the SS stood firm and although there was some bitter fighting the Poles did not break out. Meantime the SS units of von Kemp's division were heavily engaged with a powerful Polish force based on Modlin, a key fortress on the Vistula north of Warsaw. This was one of the last pockets of resistance and there was some hard fighting before it was suppressed.

Following incessant air and ground attacks, and with their supplies and ammunition exhausted, the Poles around Blonie capitulated on 17 September and the Leibstandarte resumed their advance towards Warsaw. 'Our advance took us across the battlefield. The whole area was a scene of death and destruction. The bloated bodies of men and animals blackening under the hot sun, smashed carts, burnt out vehicles and those most tragic victims of war, the wounded horses, waiting for the mercy shot...'

One by one the other islands of Polish resistance succumbed. Warsaw, facing starvation and typhoid, held out until 27 September and the forts of Modlin surrendered next day.

Hitler visited detachments of the Leibstandarte on 25 September and units of von Kempf's division the following day. Finally, with the end of the campaign, the Leibstandarte was ordered to move to Prague where the Führer's guard was accorded a rapturous reception. At the same time von Kempf's division moved back to Neidenbach near Germany's Belgian frontier. But the division was not destined for service on the Western Front as many had anticipated. It was in fact disbanded, prior to the formation of a wholly Waffen-SS division — the SS-Panzer Division Das Reich.

2

Holland
and France

SS Oberstgrüppenführer Paul Hausser (seen here as an Obergruppenführer while commanding the Das Reich Division in Russia, winter 1941) was unquestionably the ablest military commander in the Waffen-SS. After the war he sought to re-establish the reputation of the SS and claimed that the foreign units of the SS were really the precursors of the NATO army.

17

A machine gun crew in action during the Battle of France. The weapon is an MG34, called by the Leibstandarte a 'Hitler Scythe'.

Throughout the long and bitter winter of 1939-40 the Leibstandarte and the 'armed SS' or Waffen-SS — as the former Verfügungstruppe and SS-Totenkopf units were now known — trained hard for the forthcoming battles in the West. No precise details were revealed as to where and when these battles would be fought, but Hitler, who visited the Leibstandarte during December, let it be known that the SS would soon be fighting 'in regions on which their fathers' blood had been shed'.

Shortly after the Polish cease-fire a number of important organisational changes had been effected, not least of which was the creation on 10 October 1939 of the first SS field division from the three Verfügungs Standarten (1 'Deutschland', 2 'Germania' and 3 'Der Führer'). Paul Hausser was appointed its commander and at this time its official title was SS-VT Division (Motorised), although it was to become better known as 'Das Reich'. The second of the important organisational changes was initiated about a month earlier when Hitler sanctioned the formation of what was to be designated the 4th SS-Polizei Panzergrenadier Division. This formation was composed of regular police-

men (Ordnungspolizei) and during October 1939 some 15,000 police reservists were called up to fill its ranks. After a brief period of training under command of SS-Brigadeführer and Generalmajor der Polizei Karl von Pfeffer-Wildenbruch the new division moved to a concentration area in the Black Forest near Freiburg.

The third SS division — known eventually as the 3rd SS 'Totenkopf' Division — officially came into being on 1 November 1939. 6,500 of its men had been members of the infamous Theodor Eicke's Totenkopfverbände (concentration camp guards); the remainder were SS-Verfügungstruppe members and a few Allgemeine-SS (general service SS men). Eicke* was nominated commander, and the division's preliminary train-

*'Papa' Eicke had a squalid background. On Himmler's orders he had been released from a psychiatric clinic (to which he had been committed as a dangerous lunatic) to become the first commandant at Dachau and inspector of concentration camps. He was also reputed to be one of the two men who shot Ernst Röhm. By 1939 he had worked his way up the ladder to become head of the concentration camp system. Eicke is also credited with introducing the infamous skull and cross bones badge for 'Death's Head' SS units.

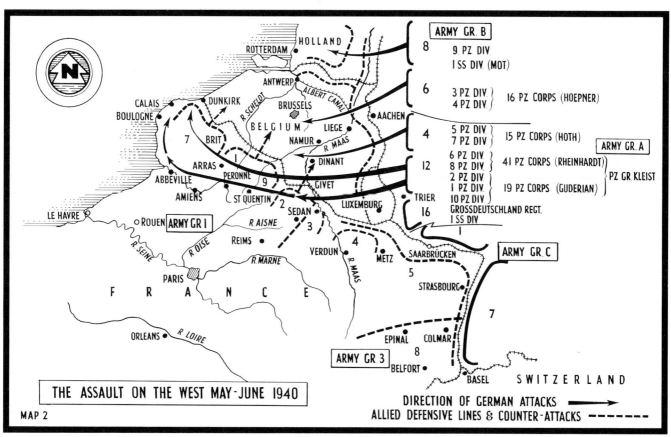

THE ASSAULT ON THE WEST MAY-JUNE 1940

MAP 2

DIRECTION OF GERMAN ATTACKS ━━▶
ALLIED DEFENSIVE LINES & COUNTER-ATTACKS ╶╶╶╶╶╶

ing was carried out at Dachau. (For this purpose the Dachau concentration camp was evacuated and its inmates transferred to camps at Flossenburg and Mauthausen until the division moved out to complete its training in Württemberg.)

Finally the raising of the first SS-Cavalry Regiment — the 1st SS Totenkopf Reiterstandarte* — deserves mention at this point, not because the regiment played any part in the fighting in Holland or France in 1940, but because it was subsequently expanded into a cavalry division which saw considerable service in Russia. The regiment was formed in Munich in September 1939 and SS-Standartenführer Hermann Fegelein took over command in November. In May 1940, when it was stationed in Poland, the regiment had 12 squadrons; six months later, while still in Poland, it was expanded and split up to create an SS cavalry brigade of two regiments.

By early May 1940 a German host of some two and a half million men — 104 infantry divisions, nine motorised divisions and 10 armoured divisions — had assembled along Germany's western borders from northern Holland to Switzerland. These were organised in three army groups: the north-

*Also unofficially known as the Fegelein Brigade — after its commander.

18
The Reichsführer-SS presents the new standard of the Liebstandarte Adolf Hitler to 'Sepp' Dietrich at Metz in September 1940.

19
A wounded member of the SS-Totenkopf Division receives medical attention during the Battle of France, 1940.

20
Members of Reichsführer-SS Himmler's staff read about the progress of the invasion of Holland, May 1940.

ernmost — Army Group B, under General Fedor von Bock — comprised two armies deployed from the North Sea to Aachen. Army Group A, under General von Rundstedt, consisted of four armies and covered a narrow zone between Aachen and Sarrebourg. Army Group C, commanded by General Wilhelm von Leeb consisted of two armies facing the French defences in Lorraine and along the River Rhine. Among this host were the two SS formations Leibstandarte and the newly created SS-VT Division; the new Polizei Division was stationed at Reutlingen and Tübingen in Württemberg and remained in reserve there until the campaign was well under way.

Up to the beginning of the month the reinforced, refurbished and refreshed Leibstandarte was concentrated west of the north German town of Osnabrück — a garrison centre well known to generations of soldiers who have served with the British Army of the Rhine.

On 8 May however both the Leibstandarte and the SS-VT Division moved up to the Dutch frontier and were poised to advance as soon as the border defences were breached. Next day, 9 May, the signal authorising the commencement of operations was received when the code-word 'Danzig' was flashed to all units of the Wehrmacht and Waffen-SS. At 0530hrs next morning a detachment of the Leibstandarte seized the bridge at De

Poppe on the frontier and opened the road for the waiting columns of Wehrmacht.

The Leibstandarte, followed by the SS-VT Division, then advanced swiftly into Holland with General Georg von Küchler's Eighteenth Army on the northern flank of the invasion. There was almost no opposition from any of the Dutch units defending this area. Road blocks were unmanned and few of the bridges along the line of advance to Rotterdam had been demolished. The first serious check came at Bornbroek where the bridge over the canal there had been blown. But the men of the Leibstandarte crossed the waterway under fire on improvised rafts, and established a bridgehead. Motorcycles were then ferried across and a detachment of SS men roared off to secure other bridges on the line of march. Meanwhile SS engineers were throwing a light bridge across the canal. By midday the Leibstandarte's advance guard had reached Zwolle, having advanced some 50 miles in six hours and captured large numbers of surprised and unprepared Dutch soldiers.

There was now a halt while the rest of the army caught up and the story is told of one Sturmmann (lance corporal) who was determined to fry some potatoes on the stove in the kitchen of a deserted farm house where he and his advance guard section had been told to settle down. Unable to get the old-fashioned stove to light by normal methods,

21
Men of the SS-Totenkopf Division receive their midday meal from a 'Gulashkanone'.

22

SS-Obergruppenführer Josef ('Sepp') Dietrich — something of an enigma. In Hitler's words: 'A man who is simultaneously cunning, energetic and brutal . . . But what care he takes of his troops.'

23, 24, 25

Men of the SS-Verfügungs Division during the campaign in France. This division subsequently changed its name to SS-Division Deutschland (December 1940), SS-Division Reich (January 1941), SS-Division Das Reich (May 1942), SS-Panzergrenadier Division Das Reich (November 1942), and finally SS-Panzer Division Das Reich (January 1944).

he fetched a can of petrol from his vehicle, poured this over the wood with which he had loaded the stove and lit it. With a great roar and a crash the fire ignited and Sturmmann Specht set to frying his potatoes. Suddenly the kitchen door burst open and in strode the company's Oberscharführer (sergeant-major). 'What the hell is going on?' he asked. 'I'm just frying some potatoes,' Specht replied. 'Do you realise you've blown the blasted chimney down?' the Oberscharführer said, 'We thought the enemy artillery had found us.'

Next morning the advance continued south to Zutphen. The demolition of two bridges across the Ijssel delayed progress, but the 3rd Battalion forced a crossing near the town and by 1400hrs they had also captured Hoven on the main north-south railway line. During this fighting SS-Obersturmführer Krass took a patrol across the Ijssel and penetrated more than 40 miles into unoccupied territory — returning with the 100 Dutch soldiers his little force had captured en route. This brought him an immediate award of the Iron Cross — the first to be awarded in the campaign.

The Leibstandarte was then transferred from the 227th Division and attached to the

9th Panzer Division, moving via Kleve and Hertogenbusch to relieve the German paratroops who had captured the huge Maas bridge and Moerdijk. From there they raced for Rotterdam in the hope of subsequently seizing the Dutch Government in The Hague. However the Dutch were now fighting back fiercely and early on 14 May the German High Command issued a verbal ultimatum. Unless the Dutch surrendered the Luftwaffe would be called upon to bomb targets in the built-up areas of Rotterdam and Utrecht. The Dutch commandant in Rotterdam refused to capitulate until he had a properly authorised document stating the German intention. The ultimatum was put in writing but meantime nobody thought to tell the Luftwaffe to delay the air strike. In the event, negotiations for a Dutch surrender were still progressing when the German bombers arrived to bomb the town.

The destruction of the business sector of Rotterdam hastened the Dutch commander's capitulation with General Kurt Student, the German airborne commander, supervising the arrangements. Two hours after the cease-fire had taken place one group of Leibstandarte SS managed to achieve a kind of fame by seriously wounding General Student as he was watching the disarming of a party of Dutch troops. An advance guard on its drive northwards to The Hague roared up and seeing hundreds of armed enemy soldiers promptly opened fire. Student was hit in the head and but for a Dutch surgeon who operated on him that night he would have died.

With the capture of Rotterdam the campaign in the Netherlands was nearly over, and the bulk of the Eighteenth Army was switched to the south to support the break-through operations that were currently being fought in northern France. The Germans had secured the right flank of their offensive and the stage was now set for phase 2 of their grand plan — separating the British and French armies prior to their destruction piecemeal in phase 3.

During the afternoon of 24 May the 1st Panzer Division, to which the Leibstandarte was now attached, had reached the Aa Canal on the eastern side of the cone-shaped zone into which the Allied armies, retreating towards Dunkirk, had been compressed. Although the SS men had had a long and tiring march, the 3rd Battalion of the Leibstandarte was ordered to capture the 42m hill, the Wattenberg, lying to the east of

the canal, which dominates the otherwise flat countryside. Shortly before the attack was due to go in, however, the tanks were ordered to halt and stand fast. The order was said to come from Hitler and therefore could not be questioned. Nevertheless it was an order which the regimental commander, SS-Obergruppenführer Sepp Dietrich, chose to ignore and the attack was launched. Under cover of a heavy artillery barrage the SS men crossed the canal, smashed their way through the French defences and captured the hill.

Spurred on by the tank commander General Heinz Guderian, the Leibstandarte continued to push forward until they were halted at Bollezelle by BEF Bren gun carriers and anti-tank guns which had been rushed up to seal off the German break-through at Watten. Meantime Hitler had quite unexpectedly rescinded his order to the armoured units. Why he did so at this particular moment remains a mystery, but Sepp Dietrich had Hitler's ear and it was perhaps because the Nazi SS was now involved that Hitler decided to relax his embargo on the employment of the armoured formations. In the event, on the morning of 28 May a combined tank-infantry force

26

27

28

26
A medical orderly attends a wounded SS man.

27
SS troops in Aire (in the Gascoigne region of France) at the end of the fighting, 30 May 1940.

28
Men of the SS-Totenkopf Division during the French campaign 1940.

29
Men of the Germania Regiment (from the SS-Verfügungs Division) in France 1940.

30
Men of the SS-Verfügungs Division receive the Iron Cross 2nd Class during the French campaign, 1940.

31
An SS medical officer inspects SS men wounded in fighting against the British during the closing stages of the battle for Dunkirk.

32
Waffen-SS men in their camouflage uniforms.

made up of the Leibstandarte, the 2nd Panzer Brigade and the 11th (Deutsche) Rifle Brigade, attacked up the Watten-Wormhoudt road.

Motoring up to coordinate the attacks of his battalion, Sepp Dietrich was cut off at Esquelberg. His car, shot up by men of the 5th Battalion The Gloucestershire Regiment, caught fire and Dietrich and his adjutant had to hide in a ditch to wait for the Leibstandarte men to rescue them. Attacks by two companies of infantry and another supported by armoured vehicles failed to break through to the SS commander, and a full battalion assault had to be mounted before a patrol could bring Dietrich and his adjutant out. Dietrich said afterwards that

the British defence of Esquelberg was the most severe opposition that the SS encountered and he and his men thought that they were up against first-class regular troops. The fact that he had had to take shelter at a critical stage of the battle subsequently saved Dietrich from being charged as an accessory to a war crime. At the village of Wormhoudt, 17 miles from Dunkirk, a handful of men from the Royal Warwickshires stubbornly resisted the Leibstandarte's effort to clear the route to their objective. Mounting casualties infuriated the SS men and in the following 24 hours men of the Leibstandarte massacred between 60 and 80 British prisoners-of-war in a particularly barbarous manner. After herding the prisoners — including wounded

30

29

— into a barn, the SS men lobbed hand grenades into the building.* Some of the wretched prisoners tried to break out and escape, but they were pursued and killed in cold blood. Only a handful of British, left by the Germans for dead, survived to tell the story of the Wormhoudt massacre. In the event Sepp Dietrich was able to say in all honesty five years later: 'I spent the day in a ditch. I saw nothing of any shooting.'

Oddly enough Dietrich is said to have showed an uncharacteristic old-fashioned courtesy to some of the other British prisoners captured in the Wormhoudt action — presenting them with SS badges and flashes as souvenirs. About the time he was doing so further down the road in the mining village of Divion-en-Artois a patrol of his troops was making sure that a British chaplain, the Reverend Reginald Podmore, whom they had cut down with a burst of machine gun fire would not live to report that they had shot a non-combatant.*

The Leibstandarte was not the only SS formation whose troops committed atrocities. When the campaign opened on 10 May, the SS Totenkopf Division was being held as part of the Wehrmacht's reserve in Germany, near Kassel. On 16 May it was ordered to exploit the salient created by the advancing German armour. In consequence the Totenkopf dashed through Belgium to fill the gap between von Reichenau's Sixth Army and Kluge's Fourth along the Maas. The division arrived on 19 May and was immediately instructed to clean up the enemy positions and consolidate the area of Le Cateau and Cambrai. However, in order to ease the pressure on the ever shrinking Allied perimeter of the retreating British Expeditionary Force, its commander Lord Gort attempted a counter-attack. The counter-attack failed but there was heavy fighting before the Germans were able to resume their advance towards the Channel ports. In the course of this fighting on 27 May 1940, men of the 4th Company of the 1st Battalion of the 2nd SS Totenkopf Regiment under command of Sturmbann

*The same method of extermination was reputedly used again four years later by men of the SS Das Reich Division (the name given to the SS-VT Division of 1940) when more than 500 French civilians were killed in a church at Oradour-sur-Glane.

†Podmore had gone back to the village to collect some of his kit. His vehicle was stopped by a burst of fire which also severed his legs. The SS men are believed to have refused medical assistance and the padre died on the pavement.

führer Fritz Knöchlein executed 100 men of the 2nd Royal Norfolks after they had surrendered at Le Paradis — a little village in the Pas-de-Calais area. (Knöchlein was subsequently hanged by the British for this crime.)

The division was pulled out of the fighting four days after this incident, sent to the Channel coast south of Dunkirk, and deployed for coastal defence around Gravelines. The men were tired so a few days occupied mainly on guard duty came as a welcome respite. One SS veteran recounts how during this period he fell asleep while guarding a bridge — a heinous offence. However he was woken up by someone shaking his shoulder and saying, 'Hullo, good evening!' It was a British soldier and on the road nearby was a British vehicle. Maybe the British soldier was as surprised as the SS man when he realised the identity of the sentry. In the event he merely turned on his heel, climbed into his truck and drove away. And, for his part, the astonished sentry was happy to see him go.

From Gravelines the Totenkopf moved some 50 miles south to the St Pol region and then when General Paul von Kleist's armour started to push from the Marne on 12 June, the division joined the advance and swept through central France across the Seine and

down to the Loire. Following the fall of Paris on 14 June, the real fighting in the battle of France was over and the Totenkopf was occupied merely in rounding up prisoners. Finally, on 25 June, the day after the cease-fire, the division was sent to occupy a sector of the French coast just north of the Spanish frontier. There the SS-Totenkopf Division remained until the end of April 1941 when it received orders to move east.

Meantime the SS-VT Division and the Leibstandarte Regiment had both been in the thick of the fighting. From Rotterdam the men of the Leibstandarte had advanced to the sea at Boulogne. They were then pulled out of the line and were resting in billets at Etrepilly on 14 June when the news that Paris had fallen was relayed to them; in a fever of elation the SS rang the bells of the village church.

The campaign was now a pursuit; there was little more serious fighting as the German columns raced southwards through France. Only at one point was the headlong rush of the Leibstandarte checked — albeit temporarily. On 19 June the advance guard came to a bridge across the Sioule River at St Pourrain where French troops were frantically trying to build a barricade. Realising that success depended on surprise and quick action the commander of the motorcycle detachment at the head of the advance guard ordered SS-Obersturmführer Knittel to rush the bridge. Covered by machine gun fire from a couple of reconnaissance vehicles and a mortar section accompanying the advance guard, Knittel's motorcyclist roared down the road to capture the barricade. No sooner had they done so however than the bridge was blown up and the Leibstandarte had to find an alternative place to cross the Sioule. This was done very quickly by the leading company of the Leibstandarte's 3rd Battalion — commanded by a certain Joachim Peiper (he preferred to be called Jochen), who was one of the youngest regimental commanders in the German Army and who achieved fame four years later in the so-called Battle of the Bulge.

The Leibstandarte's 2nd Battalion led the chase next day and by the late afternoon the SS men had captured the airfield at Clermont-Ferrand together with a vast haul of planes, eight tanks and thousands of prisoners. On 24 June the signing of an Armistice bringing the campaign to an official close the following day found the Leibstandarte in St Etienne. This was part of what became Vichy France, and the regiment moved into the German-occupied zone of France and finally to Metz where it remained until the spring of 1941, training hard for the next campaign. In August 1940 the Leibstandarte was expanded to brigade strength and a new colour presented. 'It will be an honour for you, who bear my name', declared the Führer on this occasion 'to lead every German attack'.

Like the Totenkopf Division, the SS-VT Division was attached to Kleist's Panzergruppe and participated in the main drive to Paris. By the end of the battle of France the division had advanced all the way to the Spanish frontier. It remained at Vesoul in occupied France until March 1941, training for the impending invasion of Britain. Meanwhile further organisational changes were being effected. At the beginning of December 1940 its name was changed to SS-Division 'Deutschland'. However, it soon became obvious that this name was confused with that of Germany's oldest and most famous regiment and so at the end of January 1941 the division was redesignated SS-Division 'Das Reich'.

Finally mention must be made of von Pfeffer-Wildenbruch's Polizei Division which had barely shaken down as an organised formation by the time the campaign in the West opened. Because the division was not considered to be an elite formation — certainly not so far as the SS were concerned* — it was not issued with the latest and best equipment. When France was invaded the Polizei Division was held in reserve at Reutlingen and Tübingen in Württemberg. The Division was equipped solely with horse transport and was therefore unable to operate with the fast moving tank formations. Its first taste of action came only on 9 June when it was employed in assault crossings of the River Aisne at the Ardennes Canal. Once the objectives were secured in this area the division moved on to the Argonne Forest where it fought a tough battle to capture the town of Les Islettes. On 20 June 1940 the division was pulled out and put in reserve and it remained in France until it was transferred to East Prussia in June 1941.

*Although subordinate to Himmler, the Reichsführer SS and Chief of German Police, members of the Polizei Division were not obliged to meet the racial and physical requirements demanded of SS men. At this time, therefore, they were not considered SS men and they wore the uniform of the Ordnungspolizei with the Army eagle on the sleeve.

3
The Balkans
1941

Many historians believe that Germany could have defeated the Soviet Union in 1941 if the launching of *Unternehmen Barbarossa* (Operation 'Barbarossa' — the invasion of Russia) had not been delayed by the Balkan campaign. But the campaign was necessary to bale out Italy, Germany's ally. In October 1940 Mussolini had decided to invade Greece. Greece counter-attacked, driving the Italian forces back into Albania (an Italian satellite) and Hitler had to go to the aid of his fellow dictator.

Planning for the campaign — Operation 'Marita' — began in late 1940 and two German armies, the Second and the Twelfth, were moved up in readiness. The SS Division Das Reich was attached to Baron von Weiss's Second Army and the Leibstandarte formed part of General Siegmund W. List's Twelfth Army. The plan was to persuade Hungary, Rumania and Bulgaria to cooperate in allowing German troops to pass through their territory into Greece; all three countries promised cooperation, and Bulgaria let German advance parties dressed in civilian clothes move into the country. Diplomatic pressure was brought to bear on Yugoslavia at the same time, and on 25 March 1941 Paul, the Prince Regent of Yugoslavia, also agreed to cooperate with Germany and her Italian ally. However a coup on the following night put the 17-year old King Peter in power, Paul had to flee and Yugoslavia renounced her agreement to cooperate. So Yugoslavia now had to be included in Operation 'Marita'.

The Leibstandarte was one of the first formations to move into position for the coming

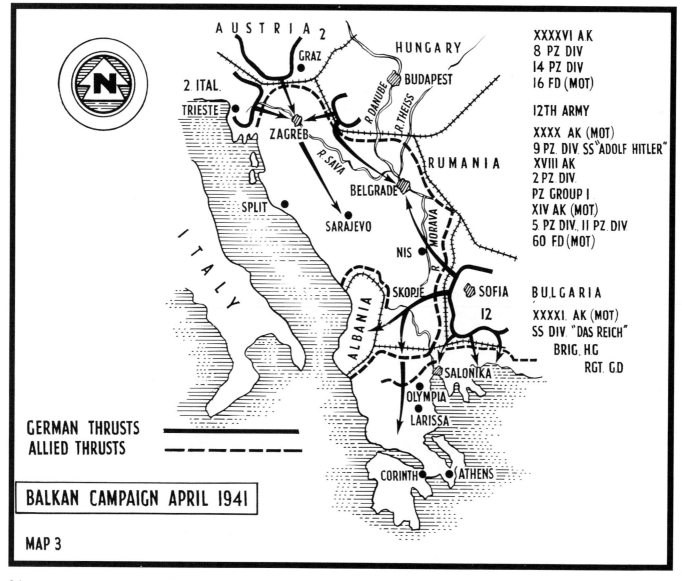

GERMAN THRUSTS ———
ALLIED THRUSTS - - - - -

BALKAN CAMPAIGN APRIL 1941

MAP 3

XXXXVI A.K
8 PZ DIV
14 PZ DIV
16 FD (MOT)

12TH ARMY

XXXX AK (MOT)
9 PZ. DIV. SS "ADOLF HITLER"
XVIII AK
2 PZ. DIV.
PZ GROUP I
XIV AK (MOT)
5 PZ. DIV., 11 PZ DIV.
60 FD (MOT)

BULGARIA

XXXXI. AK (MOT)
SS DIV. "DAS REICH"
BRIG. HG
RGT. GD

offensive. Leaving Metz at the beginning of February 1941 it travelled via Campelung in Rumania to Bulgaria from where the Twelfth Army was to advance towards Skoplje in southern Yugoslavia. The SS Division Das Reich did not move up until a few days before the end of March. Once the order was received however, the motorised division sped through Munich, Vienna and Budapest on to Temesvar on the Rumanian-Yugoslav border.

Hostilities opened on 6 April. Preceded by bombing raids which concentrated on Belgrade (Beograd) German armoured infantry columns slashed into Yugoslavia from north, south and south-east in the familiar blitzkrieg style. The Das Reich Division was with the force thrusting down from the north to take Belgrade. Hasty efforts to mobilise the million-man Yugoslav army were never completed. Zagreb fell to a combined attack by armoured units and SS men

33
Germanic volunteer in the Nordland Regiment is trained in the use of a light mortar, 1941.

34
Clothing inspection in the SS barracks in Prague, 1940.

35, 36, 37
These photos illustrate the daily routine followed by SS officers and men of the SS-Standarte I Deutschland (the first of the three infantry regiments of the Verfügungs Division) while stationed in Prague during 1939-40.

35

of Das Reich on 10 April, and Belgrade surrendered to an SS assault group from Das Reich on 13 April. There had, in fact, been keen competition between the SS division and the elite Grossdeutschland Regiment who got to the Yugoslav capital first. Sheer audacity gave the SS men the prize. Most of the roads into the city were blocked and guarded by Yugoslav troops, but SS Hauptsturmführer Klingenberg with the aid of a 'liberated' Yugoslav motorboat led a party of motorcycle riflemen across a river on a round-about route which eventually took them into the suburbs of Belgrade. There was little opposition and having reached his objective Klingenberg set about finding the mayor — from whom he demanded the surrender of the city. Belgrade had been subjected to round-the-clock bombing for a week by this time and the mayor, like most of the inhabitants of the city, had had enough. So Belgrade surrendered and Klingenberg was subsequently awarded the Knight's Cross for his daring.

One story of this period worth recounting is of a soldier trying to bilk simple peasants and vice versa. Yugoslav in 1941 was a poor country and at least one Yugoslav peasant saw an opportunity for some profitable bartering when the Germans invaded their country. Approaching a German column

halted by the roadside he managed to convey to a group of SS men that he wanted flints — the sort of flints that are used in cigarette lighters. In exchange for a reasonable quantity of flints he would hand over the block of tobacco he was carrying. The block was passed around; it smelled deliciously of Latakia. 'We'll have to have this,' one of the SS men said. 'But where the hell will we get flints?' asked another. 'Leave it to me,' said a third, and he disappeared into one of the vehicles. There it seems he found a piece of rusty wire of about the same diameter as that of a flint; this, he cut up. Returning to the group he handed over the 'flints' and the peasant duly gave him the block of tobacco. When the SS men came to examine it they found that the block was mainly straw. Only the thin outside leaves were tobacco . . . the diddlers had themselves been diddled!

When the campaign opened the SS Brigade Leibstandarte was concentrated on the Rumanian-Yugoslav border in the vicinity of Kustendil, poised for the dash to Skopje some 60 miles inside Yugoslavia. Within 24 hours the 9th Panzer Division supported by the Leibstandarte had achieved their objective and by 9 April the Leibstandarte, spearheading the German advance in this region, was heading south with orders to force the Monastir Gap, the

38
Hungarian officers watch men of the SS Division Das Reich racing through Budapest on their way to Yugoslavia in April 1941.

39
SS troops using an improvised ramp to get their transport down an obstacle impeding their advance in Greece during April 1941.

40
'Sepp' Dietrich leaves the Greek HQ at the Hotel Acropole in Jannina following the capitulation of the Epirus Army, 29 April 1941.

38

3,000ft high Javat Pass, 20 miles west of Monastir (Bitola). The Monastir Gap is known as the gateway to Greece and the Leibstandarte's 1st Battalion, with field and anti-tank artillery and a company of engineers, was given the task of breaking through. When the SS battalion reached the Greek frontier it was dusk. As the passes which constituted the battalion's objective a few miles further on were known to be defended, the battalion commander decided to mount a dawn attack. It was snowing heavily and a bitterly cold night; in consequence the troops spent a miserable night before going into action. Next day there was some stiff fighting at the Klidi Pass where the mountain crests dominating the pass were firmly held by British and Australian troops. The SS men eventually broke in, however and there was a good deal of hand-to-hand fighting before the British were driven from their positions. By midday on 12 April the Klidi Pass was in German hands together with some 80 of the 600 prisoners that were to be captured in this battle. Most of these prisoners were from the Australian

2nd/4th Battalion and were the first Imperial troops the Leibstandarte had come into contact with: '... They do not behave like the cold English, except in their cold arrogance and this is more external. They do not seem to be as well disciplined as the English nor do they wear their uniform as a soldier should. They were complaining of the cold for they have just arrived here from Egypt.'

Next day (13 April) the Leibstandarte drove through the pass and headed for the Klisura Pass. Emerging from its southern exit the SS men turned towards Lake Kastoria and the Kastoria Pass to strike at the Greek division protecting the British left flank. Extensive demolition slowed the pace of the advance and there was some severe fighting on the mountain slopes. Little progress was made that day. But during the night battle groups from the Leibstandarte's Reconnaissance Battalion, under SS-Sturmbannführer Kurt Meyer, managed to worm their way up to the crests overlooking the pass and then along goat tracks to get round the flank of the Greek positions. When dawn

41
Flemish volunteers with their
Colour parade through the streets
of Brussels, August 1941.

42
Norwegian volunteers swear their
oath of allegiance, 11 May 1942.

broke the Leibstandarte infantry renewed their attack up the mountain side and Meyer's men charged in from the rear. The Greek defences fought back with savage determination but their resistance crumbled under the pressure of the SS men's assault. Within a matter of hours the road was open and hundreds of Greek prisoners were tramping into captivity.

Following a brisk action resulting in the capture of Kastoria by the Leibstandarte's 3rd Battalion, the advance was then directed south to Gravena and from there to Ioannina. With the capture of the Mesovan Pass on 21 April the Greek troops on the western side of the Pindus mountains were cut off and next day the Greek First Army surrendered. Meanwhile the British force in Greece was retreating southwards along the Aegean coast towards Athens. The Leibstandarte followed in hot pursuit. In an endeavour to cut off the British the SS formation took a westerly route from Ioannina, driving south to Arta then over the Pindus mountains to reach the Strait of Corinth at Navpaktos — only to find that the British had eluded them by evacuation. Meyer, the Reconnaissance Battalion commander, commandeered some fishing boats at Navpaktos and ferried the advance guard across to the Peleponnese. The rest of the

The Danish Free Corps return
from the Eastern Front to a rough
reception in Copenhagen, August
1942.

Leibstandarte followed and on 27 April the
3rd Battalion moved down the west coast
road to Pirgos where the battle group
captured a party of men of the 3rd Royal
Tank Regiment. Meanwhile another battle
group — from Meyer's Reconnaissance
Battalion — was clearing the southern coast
of the Gulf of Corinth and linking up with
paratroops of the 2nd Fallschirmjäger Regiment who had been fighting around the
Corinth Canal. This, so far as the
Leibstandarte was concerned was the end of
the Balkan campaign. Following a victory
parade in Athens the SS troops moved back
to barracks in Czechoslovakia to refit and
prepare for their next campaign.

Brief references have been made to the
changes in the organisation and structure of
the Waffen-SS which were initiated shortly
before and during the Balkan campaign. As
these changes were to have a profound effect
it is desirable to review their background.

Before the war there were a few 'foreign'
volunteers — Norwegians, Danes, Dutch —
serving in the Verfügungsstandarte which
subsequently became the SS-VT Division

and finally the SS-Division Das Reich. But
when the Germans occupied Norway,
Denmark, Holland and Flanders many more
volunteers from these countries came
forward and it was decided to form SS-VT
regiments in which a mixture of 'Germanic'
races would serve together. Thus it was that
on 20 April 1940 — his birthday — Hitler
ordered the establishment of the SS Regiment
Norland in which Danes and Norwegians
would serve together with Germans; five
weeks later the Westland Regiment was
formed from Dutch and Flemish volunteers.
The next change came in December 1940
when the Nordland and Westland Regiments
were grouped together with the almost
exclusively German SS Regiment Germania
from the SS-VT Division*, the SS Artillery
Regiment 5 and the requisite supporting units
to form a new motorised Germania SS-Division which was eventually called SS-Div-

*This was shortly before the name of the SS-VT
Division was changed to Das Reich. As a replacement
for the loss of the Germania Regiment the SS
Totenkopf Standarte was transferred to the division
and redesignated SS-Infanterie Regiment 11.

ision Wiking. At the time of its formation the new division had little difficulty recruiting volunteers in the occupied territories; avid national socialists and those who supported the idea of Germans as the 'Master Race' rushed forward to enlist. But the volunteers' initial enthusiasm was soon curbed after a taste of service with and under Germans and the fact that some of their German masters treated them badly created considerable feelings of discontent.

In an attempt to resolve this situation and encourage more nationalists and anti-Communists from the Germanic countries to serve in the Wehrmacht and Waffen-SS it was decided that national 'legions' should be formed, composed of and commanded by volunteers from each of the west European countries occupied by Germany. (A Swedish legion was also planned in fact, and Sweden was a neutral.) This decision was made a few days after the launching of Operation 'Barbarossa' (22 June) and it marked the beginning of the second phase of Waffen-SS employment of Germanic volunteers. The legions raised in the Germanic countries were to come under the authority of Himmler's Waffen-SS; the others — from France, Wallonia and elsewhere — were to be controlled by the Wehrmacht.

Himmler and SS-Gruppenführer Gottlob Berger, the cunning and able Swabian whom

44
A contingent of Norwegian volunteers parade through Oslo, 1942.

45
SS-Brigadeführer Fritz Freitag addresses a group of Galician (Ukranian) volunteers.

Himmler had appointed chief SS recruiting officer, had high hopes for the new legions. After the fall of France it was decided to increase the size of the Wehrmacht by doubling the number of its tank divisions and this reorganisation affected the Waffen-SS. German mampower available for enlistment in the Waffen-SS was necessarily limited and so if the Waffen-SS was to maintain its current establishment let alone expand it, it had to cast its net more widely and rope in foreign recruits.

Volunteer contingents called *Freikorps* in Denmark, *Freiwilligenverband* in Norway and *Freiwillingenkorps* in the Netherlands and Belgium, were raised in the summer of 1941. Volunteers enlisted for two years or the duration of the war; they did not take the SS oath and although they were afforded the privileges and expected to accept the obligations of the SS they were not regarded as members of the SS and they did not wear the SS runes on the collars of their uniform.

In the forthcoming months the SS's foreign legions were to show that they could fight with the same courageous recklessness which characterised their full Waffen-SS comrades. Nevertheless it soon became clear that the legion concept was a failure; the legionnaires were unhappy largely because they were mismanaged by their German officers. The result was that the word got back to their homelands and the supply of new volunteers dwindled to the point when it could not keep pace with the high casualty rate sustained by the legions. So in March 1943 it was decided to break up the Germanic legions, and transfer the personnel to the Waffen-SS proper, and reconstitute the legions as bigger formations. Nobody consulted the legionnaires before the decision was taken and many of them resented the change; indeed some of them refused to be transferred and to take the SS oath*. Those that accepted the transfer formed the nucleus of the Germanic (SS) Corps — subsequently redesignated the IIIrd (Germanisches) SS-Panzer Korps, in which the principal formation was the Nordland Division. The latter was formed originally by grouping the SS-Infantry Regiment Nordland with two other Germanic legions which were brought up to strength by drafting in a large number of west and south-eastern European volunteers.

*The approximate foreign composition of the SS-Division Wiking is detailed in Appendix 4.

46

46
Dutch volunteers parade in the Hague, August 1941.

4

Operation `Barbarossa´

At 0315 hours on 22 June 1941 a thunderous artillery and air bombardment signalled the opening of *Unternehmen Barbarossa*, the invasion of Soviet Russia. Shortly afterwards Hitler's armoured units crossed the 2,000-mile front — the biggest campaign in history had begun.

Five Waffen-SS divisions took part in the invasion — the Leibstandarte and Wiking Divisions under command of von Rundstedt's Army Group South, Das Reich with von Bock's Army Group Centre, and the Totenkopf and Polizei Divisions as part of von Leeb's Army Group North. Unlike the Wehrmacht formations the SS divisions were not deployed in the concentration area in Poland until the eleventh hour and the Polizei Division was held in reserve during the opening phases of the invasion. Even 'Hitler's Own', the Leibstandarte, did not cross the Soviet frontier until 1 July.

The Russian climate was to play a major role in the war. The date of the invasion which Hitler had originally set for the middle of May would have been right after the normal end of the spring and its muddy season. But the Balkan diversion had caused it to be postponed and the delay of a month in the start of the attack — with a con-

sequent loss of four weeks of good weather which was to lead to formidable complications. The climate of the Soviet Union west of the Volga and south of Leningrad is far from uniform, but in general the period from mid-May to the middle of September is the best, when the weather is warm and rain is not a major factor. In mid-September, however, there is the autumn mud, the dreaded *rasputitza*, as the autumn rains turn the country into a quagmire. In such conditions it was difficult if not impossible for heavy vehicles to move over the primitive Russian roads. Then in November winter sets in, and Soviet winters are bitterly cold with wind sweeping across the open steppes to add wind chill to the normal low temperatures. This necessitates special protection for men and special precautions for vehicles and weapons. SS men have recorded that bronchitis and dysentery were responsible for almost as many casualties in November 1941 as the Red Army. One individual reckoned that black ice was more of a menace at this time than the Russians. All the accounts maintain that the intense cold was a factor for which the German Army was not prepared. Winter clothing was inadequate; indeed little provision had been

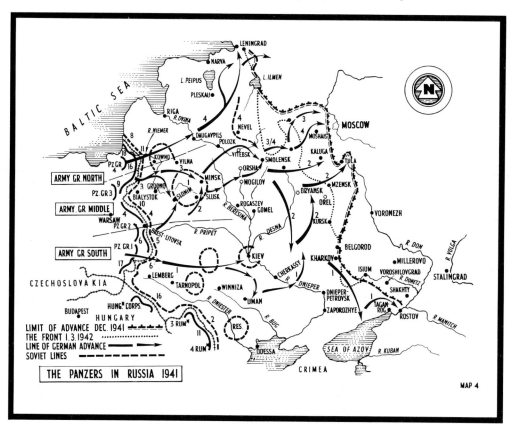

THE PANZERS IN RUSSIA 1941

MAP 4

made for a supply of it. One of the survivors of the French SS volunteer assault battalions has said that two of the French volunteers died from exposure at a temperature of −52°F while on a night patrol. (Asked how he managed to survive, this individual quoted Goethe: 'One only dies when one really want to do so'.) On another occasion the water froze in the eyes of a sentry; the man died later.

As a result of incidents like these it is easy to understand that the situation had reached a state where even fanatical SS discipline could crack. On occasions men fought to secure a sleeping place on a wooden floor in a hut, for a stout pair of boots, or a leather jacket. So far as equipment was concerned weapons were often inoperative when their working parts froze, and the engines of vehicles generally had either to be kept running continuously or restarted at very frequent intervals. If the intervals between stopping and starting was too long the engine could only be brought back to life with a blow lamp. Needless to say great care was also needed over the normal human functions, and of course when a man contracted dysentry the need to perform such functions increased.

Relief from the cold comes in March, the month in which the spring thaw starts. But the thaw brings swollen rivers and more

47
An SS officer interrogates Red Army prisoners.

48
A tank supports SS Panzergrenadiers during the bitter defensive fighting in the winter of 1943-4.

49
A wounded SS infantryman is given first aid by a tank officer of the Wiking Division, summer 1942.

50
Wiking tank crews watch an aerial attack on Soviet positions from their Panzer IIIs.

impassable *rasputitza*; this lasts until mid-May when the cycle begins again. In some parts of the Soviet Union it gets very hot in summer and an erstwhile infantryman of the Wiking Division has described conditions that his unit faced in the Ukraine in November 1942. The unit was equipped mainly with horse drawn transport; the SS men themselves marched:

'Movement in the warm sand was terribly tiring. The transport was overloaded, the wheels sank into the sand and the horses were unable to cope, so the troops were put on to push. In the end we had to give up and resort to *panje-wagons*. These are Russian carts, consisting simply of a ladder-like frame on a two-axle base with fork shafts terminating in a sort of bow which slips over the horse's neck. The wooden parts are bound together with strips of leather, and they are all easily replaceable. Like the simple sledges which the Russians use to drag loads across country the *panje-wagons* go back to the time of Ivan the Terrible. And to us they were probably just as indispensable as they were to him!

'We requisitioned our *panje-wagons* together with their drivers, some of whom were girls. And many of these Ukrainian girls — with the heads covered with gay scarves — were very attractive. Needless to say quite a few of our men tried their luck with the girls when we bivouacked for the night. [Despite instructions issued before the campaign "NOT to sleep with Russian girls for fear of venereal disease".]

'The Russian drivers were requisitioned for a week at a time. The understanding was that they would supply their services, their horses and their cart or sledge, and that we would feed them. Their ration was supposed to be the same as that of a soldier — soup, bread, salt, potatoes, milk, eggs and "speck" (the potatoes, milk and eggs having been liberated from the locals by the *Wiking* supply service, of course). In fact, the drivers serving with the LVF (Legion of French Volunteers) generally did better, because we believed in sharing everything . . .'

Apart from the Russian climate the Germans also suffered from the activities of partisan

51
Members of the Leibstandarte in their newly issued winter uniforms. The stripe on the sleeve was to help identify friend from foe, winter 1941-2.

52

53

forces operating in the German rear. These guerilla fighters tied down whole divisions of troops and committed acts of sabotage and atrocity against the Germans. In regions where the local population had come to terms with the occupying forces such acts were intended to provoke retaliation, so upsetting the locals and the Germans. This behaviour helped to develop the harshness, the brutality and the contempt for human life which characterised the war on the Eastern Front. It was probably never possible to establish who was responsible for the first atrocity but it is certain that a special hatred was engendered between the Waffen-SS and the Russians, and Soviet hatred was particularly strong against men of the Leibstandarte who wore the cuff band 'Adolf Hitler'. Within days of the start of the campaign the men of the Leibstandarte were convinced that their wounded who had fallen into enemy hands had been summarily and brutally executed. (This attitude had a parallel in Normandy where the Canadians believed the same of the Hitler Jugend.) In the event this gave rise to the practice of SS officers administering the *coup de grace* to wounded men who could not be evacuated from the battlefield, in order to save them

from torture. In Russia life was not held to be so dear and the SS summarily shot partisans, commissars and any others who were uncooperative or suspected of sabotage. It is hardly surprising therefore that the SS soon gained the reputation of being able to pacify a district where there was partisan activity more quickly and more effectively than the Wehrmacht.

On occasions it seems that even the SS were judged to have gone too far in the battles against partisans. Even so, the individuals concerned usually got away with little more than a mild reprimand. One SS officer who was arraigned before a court-martial charged with responsibility for the murder of Soviet peasants was acquitted. His defence was based on a quotation from Hitler's *Mein Kampf*: 'Terror is suppressed only by terror.'

The first phase of the war against Russia started with the opening battles of Operation Barbarossa and terminated in June 1942. Army Group Centre, which included the Das Reich Division, advanced spectacularly and its armoured pincers closed on Minsk by mid-July, then opened in another scoop as the German tanks crossed the Dnieper. In August 1941 *Das Reich* took part in the

54

52
Waffen-SS military police rounding up partisans and searching Red Army stragglers, July 1941.

53
An SS military policeman inspects a Soviet semi-automatic rifle found during the search for red army stragglers, July 1941.

54
SS troops in action.

battle of Yalnya east of Smolensk which resulted in the capture of 100,000 Russian prisoners. The Russian armies recoiled in disorder and the German spearheads reached Beloj, less than 200 miles west of Moscow. However Army Group South with the Leibstandarte and Wiking Divisions had made slower progress. The German supply system was strained to breaking point by the immense distances while tanks and other vehicles were beginning to show the strain of the terrific pace and long marches. The advance of Army Group North, impeded as it was by difficult terrain, was even slower than that of Army Group South. In the initial phase of the campaign the SS-Polizei Division was held in reserve but in August 1941 this division and the Wehrmacht's 269th Infantry Division launched a combined attack on the heavily fortified Soviet position at Luga which blocked the road to Leningrad. The approach to the objective was through forest and swamp and the Russians contested every inch of ground. The result was that the SS-Polizei had suffered more than 2,000 casualties in killed and wounded even before the actual attack went in. There was a brief pause while three other Wehrmacht divisions moved up and then a combined assault was launched. It was entirely successful although it cost the SS-Polizei many more casualties. Meanwhile the units of the SS-Totenkopf had been fighting

their way up along the Lithuanian border, against stiffening resistance into Latvia. After the elimination of the Luga bridgehead both SS divisions moved up to invest Leningrad and in the second week of August the Totenkopf broke through the Russian line, to capture Chudovo on the main Leningrad to Moscow railway.

With Army Group South the Wiking was 'blooded' at Tarnopol in Galicia at the end of June. Soon after this the Leibstandarte ran into trouble in an operation to capture an important road junction on the way to Kiev. The SS men stormed their objective but the Russians launched a furious counter-attack. 'These must have been elite troops ... nearly as good as us,' recorded a member of the Leibstandarte before going on to describe the Red Army's fanatical attitude, as expressed in bayonet charges and savage hand-to-hand fighting. 'We trained for close combat back in the golden days, although we always thought it somewhat superfluous. We don't now ... these are the best fighters we have ever met ... better even than the Poles!' Much of this particular battle was fought out in the dark, with the SS and Russians stabbing and hacking at each other in the forest, while mortar bombs rained down on both sides. According to Obersturmbannführer Kurt Meyer — nicknamed 'Panzer' Meyer, who later commanded the Hitlerjugend Division in Normandy — the losses suffered

56
An SS assault gun crew go for
the plan of attack, winter
1942-3.

57
SS-Gruppenführer Steiner,
commander of the SS Wiking
Division and, later, commander of
the 3rd SS-Panzer Corps.

58
The Leibstandarte enters burning
Mariupol on the way to the Azov
Sea, October 1941.

59

59
SS reconnaissance battalion advances into the Ukraine, June 1941.

60
Weary SS grenadiers in the ruins of a Soviet town, winter 1941-2.

61
Street fighting in a Soviet village. An SS infantryman in action, summer 1942.

60

during this battle exceeded the total casualties suffered by the division in all the other campaigns.

The objective of the original plan was Kiev, the Ukrainian capital, but Hitler changed his mind and directed that the Sixth Army should wheel south and seize Uman and Nova Archangelsk. The German armoured columns swung out to encircle and contain the Soviet troops defending these towns. Twenty-five divisions were trapped in the pocket when the Germans had completed their encirclement and there was bitter fighting as the Russians desperately tried to break out. The ring held but counter-attacks were heavy and continuous: 'We are exhausted from lack of sleep,' wrote one of the Leibstandarte men. 'We seem to have been fighting without adequate sleep for weeks now ... I've lost all track of time ... Yesterday their cavalry charged our recce vehicles just after we had driven off an attack by their armoured cars ...' A stronger attack supported by tanks succeeded in smashing a gap in the SS lines but a Leibstandarte battalion counter-attacked and restored the situation:

'Our attack was met by an inferno of fire as the Russians showered us with everything they had. Here and there a man wavered. But soon they were scorning all cover and standing erect above the waving corn which provided the enemy with such excellent

camouflage. Now, whenever a Russian helmet appeared above the yellow sea German rifles cracked. It was more like a rat hunt than a battle, except that the quarry also held rifles. Our men literally stood face to face with death in the cornfield. In the middle of it all a Russian stood up and waved a German helmet. "They're giving up, they're cracking," the men shouted and began to advance with their rifles dropped. But the lieutenant was wary. "Keep down!" he called and hobbled forward alone towards the would-be deserter. At that moment two Russian machine guns opened up on the men diving for cover. Roused to fury by this trick, our men drove the attack relentlessly forward, ever closer to the cunning enemy. A bitter struggle developed, man against man, between the Germans upright in the corn and the Russian crouching at bay in his hole. At the right moment two self-propelled guns arrived in our sector, and carried the attack farther forward.

'One man was severely wounded in the chest. His section commander saw it and immediately dropped beside him, tore open his field-dressing and started to bind up the wound. Hardly had he started when he was spotted by a Red Army man, and shot through the head in the middle of his act of mercy.

'Our enraged men gave way neither to the enemy's terrible fire nor to his treacherous cunning, and before long the hill was in our hands.'

In this same action one of the SS men waved to a Russian, whom he saw getting to his feet in the corn, to come over and surrender. The Red Army man grinned, moved a few steps closer and then, with a quick movement pulled out a hand-grenade and threw it at the German, who, lucky for him, had the presence of mind to throw himself flat on his face into the corn. Another SS man saw it happen, and fired at the Russian but only wounded him. Then the first man beckoned to him again to come over and give himself up, but he smiled absentmindedly, pulled out another grenade and put it under his chin. The account continued:

'Later we were told by some prisoners that this man was the last surviving commissar of the regiment which we had knocked about so severely in the fighting of the last two days.

'But not all political commissars were so obdurate nor yet served their masters so abjectly as that fanatic. We had several times come across boxes containing complete civilian outfits, down to shirts, shoes, ties and even cloth caps. They puzzled us for a long time until we were eventually let into the secret by a soured and embittered prisoner. Apparently most of the commissars had provided themselves, secretly of course, with one of these boxes which they hoped would give them a chance of getting away safely if things did finally go wrong. These "funk boxes" of Stalin's political commissars said little for the communist belief in victory. "Fight to the last drop of blood, comrade. Hey, Ivan, where's my box?" '

Following these battles another 100,000 Russian soldiers marched into captivity and the part played by the Leibstandarte in the action was acknowledged by the corps commander, General Werner Kempf. He wrote: 'Since 24 July the Leibstandarte SS Adolf Hitler has taken the most glorious part in the encirclement of the enemy around Uman. Committed at the focus of the battle for the seizure of the key enemy position at Archangelsk, the Leibstandarte... with incomparable dash, took the city and the heights to the south. In the spirit of the most devoted brotherhood of arms, they intervened on their own initiative in the arduous struggle... Today at the conclusion of the battle of annihilation around Uman I want to recognise and express my special thanks to the Leibstandarte SS Adolf Hitler for their exemplary effort and incomparable bravery.'

62, 63
Members of the Leibstandarte are decorated for their bravery in the fighting on the Eastern Front, summer 1942.

64
SS Panther tanks advance eastwards from the Bug.

64

With the fall of Uman the advance continued in a south-easterly direction to Nikolayev and then to Cherson, a large industrial city where there was some intensive street fighting between SS men and Soviet Marines before the town fell. The German advance then continued east to the Dnieper which the Wiking Division crossed near Dnepropetrovsk on 21 August prior to continuing the advance towards Rostov. In the first week of September the Leibstandarte also crossed the river and headed for Rostov across the Nogai Steppe. This is a vast depressing wasteland and one SS man recorded:

'There is very little water and what there is is salty. Coffee tastes of salt, the soup seems to be full of salt . . . but we are pleased to get even this tepid liquid because this is true desert country. Movement is visible for miles; clouds of choking, red brown dust hang over our columns when we are moving, and pinpoint our exact positions. Paradoxically

67

68

65, 66, 67, 68, 69
Panzergrenadiers in action on
the Eastern Front during 1942.

69

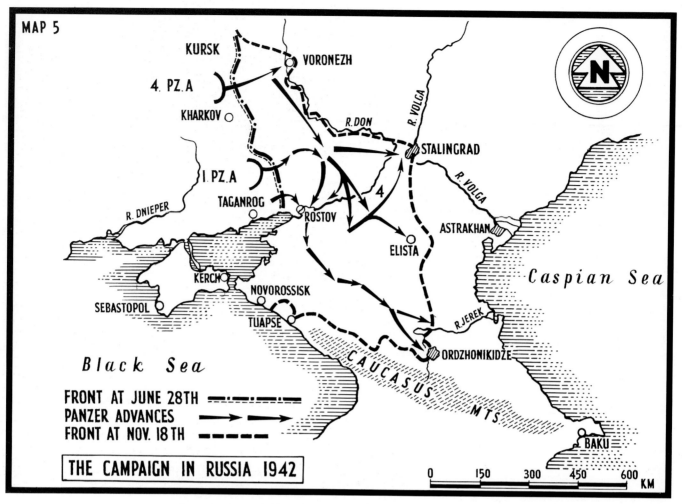

MAP 5

KURSK

VORONEZH

4. PZ.A

KHARKOV

R.DON

R. VOLGA

STALINGRAD

R. VOLGA

I. PZ.A

TAGANROG

ROSTOV

4

ASTRAKHAN

R. DNIEPER

ELISTA

KERCH

Caspian Sea

SEBASTOPOL

NOVOROSSISK

TUAPSE

R. JEREK

Black Sea

CAUCASUS

ORDZHONIKIDZE

MTS

FRONT AT JUNE 28TH ▬▬▬

PANZER ADVANCES ➔ ➔

FRONT AT NOV. 18TH ▬ ▬ ▬

BAKU

THE CAMPAIGN IN RUSSIA 1942

0   150   300   450   600

KM

the only signs of life are the dead tree trunks of telegraph poles. Without them it would be difficult to orientate oneself . . . sometimes we find a melon field and gorge ourselves, but the unripe fruits have unhappy effects . . .'

As the advance continued towards Rostov there was some violent hand-to-hand fighting for villages en route, which Russian troops defended with unbelievable tenacity. But when the shooting stopped the German troops were often greeted quite cordially. Indeed many of the Russians in the early days of the invasion regarded the Germans as liberators. There was a good deal of fraternisation in the rear areas, the Germans were billeted with Soviet families. Pretty Russian girls were taken into their beds and other not-so-pretty girls cooked for them and washed their clothes. In those early days there was no sabotage nor even partisans, although a strict curfew was enforced, precluding the civilian population from being on the streets after dark.

Morale in many of the Soviet units was low at this stage of the war and the German advance was often hampered by the need to cope with large numbers of Red Army deserters. The commander of a Leibstandarte reconnaissance detachment has described how the people in one village on the shores of the Sea of Azov on the road to Rostov were happy to cooperate with the invaders:

'The last Red troops had moved through the village three hours before. "They went that way" — a woman pointed out.

'We drove slowly through the village. Men and women brought us milk and melons.

'The ripening harvest received us again: vineyards, orchards, fields of tall maize. And then the second village. When we drove in — more precipitately than I should have permitted — found the place swarming with Red Army men. The despatch-rider behind heard the screech of our brakes, saw the first brown uniforms, turned like a flash and was gone. The second followed close behind him. In a cold fear I got down to the road and the man beside me raised his tommy-gun. But at that moment a tall Ukrainian walked up to us. "*Vudyna kaputt* — the war's over." Then he complained that the peasants were refusing to provide food for his hungry men. I had all rifles, machine guns and mortars collected into a pile and then sent for the village headman. There was none. "Right, then you're it", and I pointed to an old man. He was flattered and smiled. As it happened, I had picked the right man; he had done five years' forced labour for refusing to join the collective farm and had a very healthy hatred of the Bolsheviks. There was soon food for our hungry prisoners. Before very much longer the whole battalion came racing up, expecting to find nothing but our bodies, and there was general rejoicing when they found that we had come to no harm.'

For the invaders the problems of October and November 1941 could be summarised as time, space and 'General Mud'. Army Group North with the Totenkopf and Polizei Divisions bogged down in front of Leningrad. Army Group Centre was reinforced and in November Das Reich Division spearheaded the long delayed assault on Moscow. The new offensive got off to a good start, with a tremendous victory at Vyasma when more than 650,000 prisoners were taken. Rain now slowed the advance, however, although the drive continued and by mid-October the Germans were within 40 miles of the Soviet capital. An all-out effort was called for and again Das Reich took the lead, to effect a

70
SS men prepare a meal while travelling by train to the front, Russia 1942.

71
An SS tank unit resting, Russia 1942.

deep penetration into the Moscow defences south of Borodino. But the cost was appalling; Das Reich alone was down to a combat strength of 60% by mid-November.

Meantime, Army Group South with the Leibstandarte and Wiking Divisions had launched an attack on Rostov. The fighting was now in the biting cold of a Russian winter. Leibstandarte Scharführer Erich Klein remembered:

'The nights were indescribable. We had neither greatcoats nor proper winter underclothing and most of us did not even have gloves. We lay in the Russian trenches, our heads scantily covered with tarpaulins stiff with ice, while outside the howling blizzard drove great waves of powdered snow before it. Many froze to death. To urinate caused unspeakable agony and any sheltered corner or hut we could find was used as a latrine rather than as living quarters.

'On the third day of our attack, a dense blanket of fog covered the ice-bound country and visibility was barely three yards. All round us we could hear the grinding of tank tracks. Slowly and cautiously we groped our way forward into the thick brew, halting every few minutes to listen. Finally, after we had once again managed to lose contact on both flanks, we were halted altogether. The fog lifted a little, but it was still impossible to see more than 20 yards. Then we heard movement ahead. Ten minutes later the unmistakable sound of marching feet came to us through the fog and, as a precaution, we

took up fire positions in the snow. The company commander had no idea what was going on and it might easily have been one of our own units, which, like ourselves, had pushed too far forward. Then the fog lifted for a moment and we distinctly saw about 500 yards in front of us, a whole regiment of tommy-gunners. That meant NKVD.

'The CO immediately gave orders to open fire and radioed frantically for help. Within a few minutes a battery of 88s came racing up and unlimbered immediately behind our lines. A cheer from the Russians sounded curiously high-pitched and shrill; they could not have been much more than boys, probably Komsomols. Despite the fury of our fire, their attack, which was made with unusual verve, came rapidly forward. The four 88s, which were firing so close over our heads that we were lifted bodily off the snow with each salvo, tore bloody lanes in the enemy attack.

'Then their attack began to waver; our company commander saw this, pulled out two platoons and led us to the counter-attack, whereupon the remainder of the Russian regiment turn and fled. As our assault swept over the first of their dead, my feet faltered. They were women, buxom young women and girls, all of about twenty. And what a terrible sight they were. The high explosive charge of the 88s had literally torn the clothes from their bodies, and they lay bundled up like discarded dolls from a puppet show. Legs torn off at the hip lay

72

73

74

72, 73, 74
SS Panzergrenadiers in action on
the Russian Front in the cold
winter weather of 1942-3.

scattered about as if in a butcher's shop, and great patches of blood coloured the blinding white of the snow. But our attack went on, on over the bodies of the women and flowing now swiftly and smoothly, carried us to the first suburbs of Rostov.'

Rostov fell and Kern said that the people greeted the Germans with 'tremendous enthusiasm'. Such enthusiasm was short-lived, however. In the event a Russian counter-attack in November drove the Germans out of the town and compelled them to fall back to defensive positions across the frozen waters of the Mius River. The Leibstandarte and Wiking Divisions held firm against furious onslaughts by the Russians. 'They came on . . . in masses so great as to numb the senses. They had to pick their way through the unburied dead of the other assaults. We drove them off — how easy it seems to write this . . . and when they had gone back the whole area in front of our positions was carpeted with dead. They were dead all right . . . the wounded die quickly; the blood freezes as it leaves the body and a sort of shock sets in which kills. Light wounds that heal in three days in summer kill you in winter . . .'

In effect the severity of the winter of 1941-2 curbed military activity along the whole length of the Russian Front, although operations did not stop altogether. In February the Russians launched an offensive with attacks from Finland in the north to the Crimea in the south and the German lines were penetrated at many points. Das Reich Division was in the thick of the fighting north-west of Moscow and by the middle of the month had suffered nearly 11,000 casualties. As a result the division was withdrawn in March and sent back to France for refitting, reinforcement and retraining. The Panzergrenadier Division Leibstandarte in the south, which had also taken a hammering, followed Das Reich to France in June.

The Wiking stayed in Russia and when the Germans returned to the offensive in July 1942 the Wiking spearheaded the attack into the Caucasian oilfields. The Polizei and Totenkopf Division also remained in Russia. The Totenkopf and the Danish legion — *Freikorps Dänemark* — attached to it, was encircled and cut off for some months near Leningrad in the so-called 'Demyansk Pocket'. During these months the division lost a lot of men and the remnants of its combat units were eventually amalgamated into a single combat group, Kamfgruppe 'Eicke'. This battle group fought its way out of the Russian encirclement in April 1942 and subsequently was withdrawn from Russia and sent to France to be reconstituted, like its sister SS divisions.

75
The Norwegian Volunteer Legion arrives at the Eastern Front near Leningrad, August 1942.

5

Russia
1943–4

Following the battering they had received in Russia, the three SS divisions, *Leibstandarte Das Reich* and *Totenkopf*, spent the second half of 1942 refitting and resting in France. The three divisions had been upgraded to Panzergrenadier status and amalgamated into a single new armoured formation, the Ist SS-Panzer Corps. Seventy five per cent of the men were recruits who needed further training, but more men were needed in Russia to bolster the crumbling German front, so they were pronounced ready for recommitment to battle. 1942 had been a traumatic year for the Germans. Hitler's fantastic changes of objectives and his insistence on an overextended offensive, and later on senseless retention of terrain, had wrecked his eastern armies. At the beginning of 1943 all the German forces in southern Russia were in jeopardy. East of Kharkov the Hungarian and Italian satellite armies

were disintegrating; the Sixth Army at Stalingrad was surrounded and in death agony; in the Don Valley in front of Rostov the Russians were threatening to cut off the First Panzer Army which was now retiring from the Caucasus.

February saw the end at Stalingrad, where the Sixth Army — food and ammunition exhausted — surrendered after a last ditch fight. But the First Panzer Army managed to reach the Don at Rostov to join General Erich von Manstein's Army Group Don. Just after the fall of Stalingrad, Manstein flew to Germany to try to get Hitler to shorten the whole Russian front. It was a vain attempt. 'All Hitler had to say about the operational situation was to express the belief that the Ist SS-Panzer Corps [which was to come under Manstein's command when it arrived in the theatre] would be able to remove the acute threat to the middle Donetz front... His

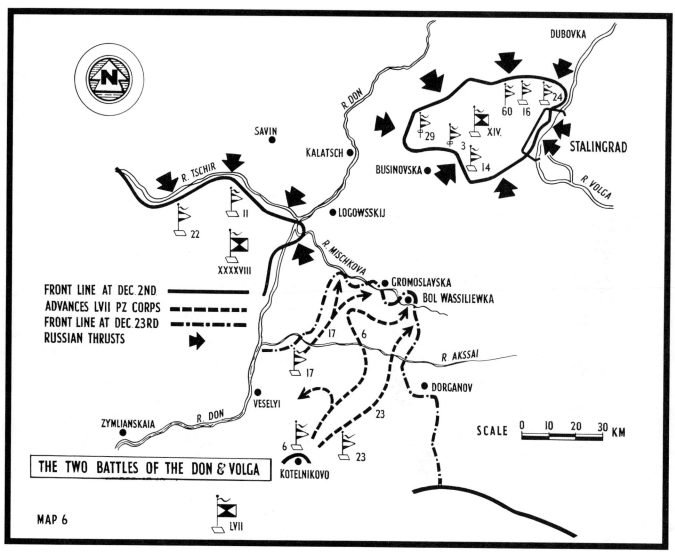

THE TWO BATTLES OF THE DON & VOLGA

FRONT LINE AT DEC. 2ND.
ADVANCES LVII PZ CORPS
FRONT LINE AT DEC. 23RD
RUSSIAN THRUSTS

SCALE 0 10 20 30 KM

MAP 6

faith in the penetrating power of this newly established SS-Panzer Corps was apparently unbounded.'

The Corps moved up to the front and was deployed with the Leibstandarte taking up a defensive position along the Donetz and Das Reich holding outposts east of the river. The front to be covered was unusually long — the sector held by the Leibstandarte at Chegevayev alone stretched for more than 70 miles and the troops were even thinner on the ground when SS Standartenführer Fritz Witt's 1st Panzergrenadier Regiment was pulled out to take part in a corps attack south-east of Alkatavka. However the remaining regiments succeeded on holding the line against an increasing tide of assaults while a confusion of retreating units — German, Italian and Hungarian — straggled through the bridgehead. Much of the fighting on the main defensive line took place in blinding snow storms.

Eventually Das Reich was compelled to fall back on the Donetz line. There the slogg-ing match continued as the SS endeavoured to hold off the Russian mass attacks. Even the wounded returned to their units to help, and one incident which occurred during this period will perhaps illustrate the character of the Waffen-SS at its best. The 320th Infantry Division, fighting its way back to the Donetz line, was surrounded. The division was burdened with 1,500 wounded whom the div-isional commander was not prepared to abandon to the Russians. The Leibstandarte was asked to help and SS-Sturmbannführer Jochen Peiper's Panzergrenadier Battalion was sent in response to the appeal. Crossing the Donetz the SS battalion penetrated more than 25 miles into Soviet-dominated territory to break through to the hard-pressed div-ision. The SS men then formed a protective screen behind which the 320th Division was able to pull back to the Donetz. However the ice on the river was too thin to bear the weight of Peiper's armoured vehicles, so — having seen the men of the 320th safely across — the SS battalion turned back into

76
SS-Gruppenführer Theodor Eicke, commander of the SS-Totenkopf Division on the Eastern Front 1942. Prior to being appointed to the command of the Totenkopf he was chief of the concentration camps. 'Papa' Eicke was shot down and killed in February 1943 near Orelka while visiting a forward unit in his Fieseler Storch.

Soviet territory and cut their way through the Russians along a circuitous route to a point where the river could be forded.

The Russian winter offensive was a body blow to the Germans but in March the Germans hit back. A counter-attack was launched with the Ist SS-Panzer Corps as its spearhead and the SS men tore a great hole in the Russian front through which the Leibstandarte and Das Reich Divisions poured. This account is from a tank driver in the Leibstandarte:

'There's nobody worse off in a tank battle than the driver. With only his narrow visor to look through, he can never see what is going on and, what is worse, can never get a real look round the battlefield. At one stage of the battle we had to turn our unprotected rear towards the enemy attack, from which position we opened rapid fire, hurling round after round against a hill. Our shells were soon falling on a white house and then at last on the forward battery that had been giving us so much trouble, and we saw debris hurled into the air. All this time I was having to shift position at ever more frequent intervals, for the remaining enemy guns were obviously concentrating all their efforts on finishing us off.

'During a short pause in the firing I took the opportunity to have a quick look round. Things were not looking too good and there must have been quite 30 of our guns and tanks on fire. There was also a healthy-looking bonfire over the enemy's side, but to make up for that at least 300 T-34s were massing against us.

'Then the loader reported: "Three more rounds to go."

'I gasped. In my excitement I had completely forgotten the need for economy and had fired off all our ammunition. Now we were in a nice mess. I swung round at once and drove over to the command tank to report. The CO said nothing. I offered to drive back and get the run restocked, but he shook his head. "Ammunition carriers will be along any moment", he said. "Try to keep going as best you can till then. And don't stay too long in any one spot, or you'll be pinpointed."

'We cruised round the battlefield for a while. Not a pleasant feeling to have to swan around uselessly and provide an Aunt Sally for the enemy. A few minutes later the driver reported laconically: "Petrol for another six miles." '

In the event this man's tank received a direct hit, and he was lucky to escape with his life. He also narrowly missed being captured.

Kharkov which the Germans had evacuated earlier was recaptured by the SS-Panzer Corps on 14 March. It was as triumph

77, 78, 79
Shots of SS Panthers in action on Eastern Front 1943.

77

80, 81
The cost of war.

for the SS men but in the battle for the town the Totenkopf's divisional commander, Theodor 'Papa' Eicke, was killed, and when the casualties were totted up the total cost in blood and bones to the SS Corps was the loss of 365 officers, and 11,154 other ranks, dead, wounded or missing: 'How pleased we all are with our success ... we have thrown them back and Kharkov is German once again. We have shown the Ivans that we can withstand their terrible winter. It can hold no fear for us again ...' (The writer was wrong — the winters of 1943-4 and 1944-5 were to promote as much fear as ever before.)

The next objective was Kursk and the battles for this town were to be the last great German offensive in Russia. As before the offensive was spearheaded by the Leibstandarte, Das Reich and Totenkopf Divisions and the plan was code-named 'Zitadelle' — 'Citadel'.

The intention was to concentrate two powerful armoured forces which would con-

82
View through the tank periscope as SS Panthers advance towards burning Lubliniz.

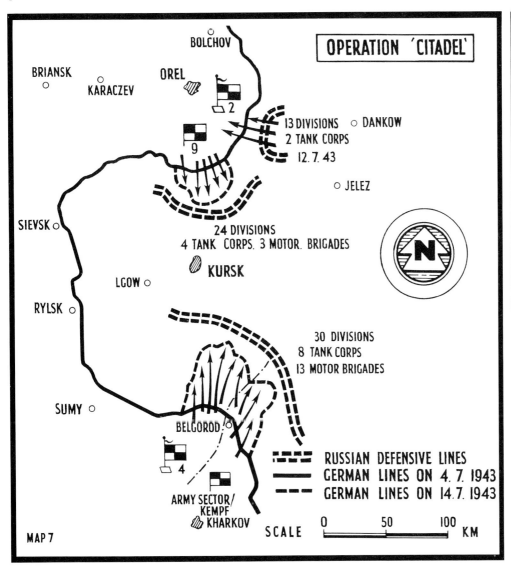

OPERATION 'CITADEL'

BOLCHOV
BRIANSK
KARACZEV
OREL
2
9
13 DIVISIONS   o DANKOW
2 TANK CORPS
12. 7. 43
o JELEZ
24 DIVISONS
4 TANK CORPS. 3 MOTOR. BRIGADES
KURSK
SIEVSK o
LGOW o
RYLSK o
30 DIVISIONS
8 TANK CORPS
13 MOTOR BRIGADES
SUMY o
BELGOROD o
4
ARMY SECTOR/
KEMPF
KHARKOV

RUSSIAN DEFENSIVE LINES
GERMAN LINES ON 4. 7. 1943
GERMAN LINES ON 14. 7. 1943

SCALE   0   50   100   KM

MAP 7

83

83, 84, 85, 86
Army and Waffen-SS troops
during the retreat from Brest-
Litowsk during the summer of
1944. (The officer in peaked cap
in photo 83 is the commander of
the Panzer Regiment 5 of the
Totenkopf Division.)

84

87

Obergruppenführer Herbert Gille seen here with SS Sturmbannführer Leon Degrelle, commander of the Belgian Volunteer Brigade Wallonien. These two led the break-out of German troops caught in the Cherkassy trap in December 1943.

88

SS troops being evacuated during the battle of Kursk.

verge on Kursk in a pincer movement designed to encircle and trap the Soviet armies in that region. The area that was to become the battlefield was a huge agricultural plain of cornfields interspersed with belts of tall steppe grass and broken by valleys and several rivers; in heavy rain the dirt roads became mud tracks. Because of this Operation 'Zitadelle' was delayed until July. 'For reasons of security', wrote one SS man immediately prior to the opening of the battle, 'We have not been allowed to move about during daytime and you can understand how hard this is, but now the waiting is over ... it is coal black outside the Command bunker. Black clouds cover the sky and the rain is streaming down. We are rested and refreshed ... the mud might slow us down but it cannot stop us. Nothing will ...'

The Battle for Kursk — the so-called 'Death Ride of the Fourth Panzer Army' —

got under way at dawn on the morning of 5 July and for a time it did indeed look as if nothing could stop the Germans. The SS-Panzer Corps divisions smashed through the forward Soviet defences with comparative ease and some daring feats of heroism were recorded. SS-Untersturmführer Michael Wittman of the Leibstandarte's 1st SS-Panzer Regiment, for example, in a Tiger, knocked out eight Soviet tanks and a number of anti-tank guns. (By the end of the battle his 'score' totalled 30 tanks and 28 anti-tank guns.) But it was not possible to continue at this rate. The Russians had a distinct tactical advantage in that the ground across which the Germans were advancing sloped gently upwards towards Kursk, giving the Russians complete observation. And as the SS men pressed on, the Russians brought down a heavy artillery barrage which slowed and finally checked the advance. Then came the Soviet counter-offensive, with the Russians hurling squadrons of tanks against single German armoured vehicles. The Russians had mobilised every person they could lay their hands on, and instances were recorded of Red Army battalions composed of civilians, without uniforms, many without boots and few having weapons but put into 'human wave' attacks to swamp the German infantry. By the end of the battle German losses were 70,000 killed or wounded, 3,000 tanks, 1,000 guns and much other war material; Russian losses in this great tank battle were probably even bigger.

Hitler told his generals that 'Zitadelle' had been 'temporarily' called off on 13 July. Three days earlier the Allies had landed in Sicily and the Führer was concerned about the stability of the Fascist regime in Italy. Plagued by the possibility of Italy's defection he ordered the transfer of the Ist SS-Panzer Corps to Italy to bolster Mussolini's position. In the event the continuing Russian offensive compelled Hitler to countermand his earlier order and only the Leibstandarte and the SS-Panzer Corps HQ were sent to Italy; Das Reich and Totenkopf remained on the Eastern Front.

Meanwhile along the whole front from Smolensk to the Black Sea the Russians were delivering a series of battering blows, featuring great masses of armour, before which the Germans steadily pulled back. Behind the German front in the occupied territory partisan activity reached a new high. Atrocities brought reprisals, and reprisals led to further atrocities. Even some of the SS

87

72

91

89, 90, 91, 92
Various shots of Waffen-SS in action on Eastern Front, c1944.

92

commanders were sickened by developments — witness a letter dated 19 July 1943 from an SS-Polizei general named Herf to his namesake, Obergruppenführer von Herff, on Himmler's staff.

'In my opinion, the reports sent out from here to the Reichsführer are "cooked". Long before I arrived people in the Ukraine were saying quite openly that our casualty reports were false. People said that the figures were kept artificially low in order to highlight the "successes". I would not wish even to hint at the reason for this. After I had been here only one day the Head of the Operations Section told me quite openly that things were going on which were not quite right. The ex-Chief of Staff (who by the way had been promised my job) told me the same thing. That was on my second day here. I have told both of them that under these circumstances I cannot remain. They advise me to try and get things changed. As you know, I have done so. Yesterday a Gauleiter and Generalkommissar unintentionally and unwittingly broadcast certain secret reports (intended for the Führer) showing that some 480 rifles were found on 6,000 dead "partisans". Put bluntly, all these men had been shot to swell the figure of enemy losses and highlight our own "heroic deeds". I am under no illusions

93, 94
SS Gruppenführer Herbert Gille of the Wiking Division and staff during the battle of Kowel.

95
A supply column in a wintry landscape.

96
Another supply column in the 'rasputitza' period.

97
An SS armoured personnel carrier equipped with flamethrower.

98, 99, 100, 101,
Tanks and SS Panzergrenadiers
in armoured personnel carriers
during the fighting in Poland in
the summer of 1944.

99

that, this being the system, the winter 1943-4 will see the beginning of the end in the rear areas and probably at the front as well. The increase in guerilla warfare is simply and solely due to the way the Russians have been treated.

'I have already on several occasions confided to you my misgivings over the "colonisation" process. If, however, we are now going to work on this system, I have no desire to see myself subsequently accused of misleading the Reichsführer-SS, with the files brought forward to prove it. The principle is that dead men there must be, no matter where they come from — otherwise the commander concerned is a bad commander and a bad soldier. What's more he won't get a decoration . . .'

Herf's prediction for the winter of 1943-4 proved correct. Taking advantage of the frozen ground the Russians launched a new winter offensive in December 1943 in the Pripet Marsh area and along the Dnieper. The Germans inflicted heavy casualties but they were forced to give up more ground. Meanwhile in the rear areas the stern measures taken to suppress the partisans had

102, 103
Tanks and SS Panzergrenadiers
in armoured personnel carriers
during the fighting in Poland in
the summer of 1944.

104
An SS tank crew during the Kursk
battles.

little real effect. In Herf's words the winter of 1943-4 was 'the beginning of the end' in Russia.

Of course the ordinary soldier had little option but to slog on, and it is perhaps appropriate to conclude this chapter with an anecdote which may serve to show that the outlook of the men of the Waffen-SS was in many ways very similar to that of our soldiers of other nations at other times.

The setting is Russia 1943, a Totenkopf Panzergrenadier battalion, and the story is told by an ex-Untersturmführer:
'After weeks of heavy fighting we were relegated to Corps reserve — which meant that at long last we could get a wash, a shave, and a proper sleep. But it didn't work out that way; in the early hours of the morning

106

107

105
SS men and Red Army prisoners carry a wounded comrade.

106, 107, 108,
Various shots of Waffen-SS in action in Russia.

108

109

110

111

109, 110, 111
Various shots of Waffen-SS in action in Russia.

112
Legions-Rottenführer Gerardus Mooyman was the first Germanic volunteer to be awarded the Ritterkreuz; he won it for the destruction of 13 Soviet tanks near Leningrad in February/March 1943.

113
Flemish volunteers swear the oath of allegiance while in the trenches facing Leningrad, December 1943.

114
Living quarters of the Dutch Volunteer Legion on the Leningrad front, December 1943.

114

there was an alert and we were called out.

'Marching up to the front one of our motorcycle dispatch riders passed my company and I noticed that his machine sounded different. "That can't be his Zündapp," I thought. Anyway, on his way back I stopped him and asked him where he got the machine. "But I've always had it, Untersturmführer," he replied. "Don't try to fool me," I said. "You had a Zündapp and now you're riding a BMW." After a certain amount of evasive stuttering and hesitation the truth came out. A Feldwebel stationed in some "cushy" post in the rear area had come up to see his Russian girl friend (*Mamuschka*) in the village where we were billeted last night. According to some of the locals he was in the habit of visiting her regularly. So, said our DR, "If that's all he needs a motorcycle for, my old Zündapp will do just as well. I can make better use of the BMW at the front!" What could I say? That night the BMW was given a coat of camouflage paint and its number plates changed. Since then, it and its rider have served us well — ferrying up ammunition, food and even our greatcoats on cold nights.'

6

Italian Interlude

In July 1943 the war in Russia flared up when the Germans attacked a Soviet salient east of the town of Kursk. The Russians checked the attack with a counter-offensive during which the largest of all tank battles of World War 2 was fought. Hitler, it seems, was less concerned with what was happening around Kursk at this time then with events in the Mediterranean. On 10 July Anglo-American armies had landed in Sicily, and on 25 July Mussolini, the Italian dictator, was summoned to the royal palace by King Victor Emmanuel, summarily dismissed from office and carted off under arrest in an ambulance to a police station.

The Führer's reaction to the news of Mussolini's downfall was one of deep shock, and his first thought was to seize those who had overthrown the Duce and restore Mussolini to power. That night he ordered that the Alpine passes between Italy and Germany and between Italy and France should be secured and some eight German divisions from France and southern Germany were hurriedly assembled for this purpose. Next morning a resourceful, intellectual SS roughneck — an Austrian by the name of Otto Skorzeny — was also summoned to the Führer's headquarters for the first time in his life and told to work out a plan to rescue Mussolini.*

The Italians under Badoglio were not expected to continue the war, but they could not suddenly turn on the Germans overnight. Hitler assumed that Badoglio would have to establish contact with the Allies to see if he could get an armistice and Allied support

*Skorzeny followed up Mussolini's rescue with an operation to kidnap the Hungarian Regent, Admiral Horthy, in Budapest in October 1944 when the latter tried to surrender Hungary to the advancing Russians.

Later he played an important, albeit controversial, role in the Battle of the Bulge — described later. His job in this operation was to organise a special brigade of 2,000 English-speaking Germans, put them in American uniforms and infiltrate them in captured US vehicles behind the American lines to cut communications, misdirect traffic and generally cause confusion. This so-called Panzer Brigade 150 achieved considerable success; about 40 jeeploads of Skorzeny's men slipped through the American lines and some posing as military police took up posts at crossroads and misdirected American traffic. A good many of these SS men caught in American uniforms were summarily shot, others were court-martialled and executed. Skorzeny himself was tried by an American tribunal at Dachau in 1947 but acquitted. After that he moved to Spain and South America where he quickly founded a prosperous business. He is now back in Germany where he is a leading light in HIAG (the ex-Waffen-SS regimental association).

115

against the German troops in Italy. This he realised would take a little time, and during that time the Führer proposed to strengthen his grip on Italy. Apart from the eight divisions rushed up to the Alpine passes, he proposed to move the Ist SS-Panzer Corps — composed of the Leibstandarte and Das Reich Divisions — from Army Group South in Russia to Italy. He believed that the politically motivated SS divisions could form a nucleus around which the Fascist elements in the Italian Army could rally. Hitler wanted to move at once even though it meant withdrawing these two key divisions from a vulnerable sector of the Front. However, after consultation with the commanders of Army Group Centre and Army Group South — both of whom were extremely loth to lose troops when they were fighting off a Russian offensive — Hitler decided to transfer only the SS-Panzer Group Headquarters and the Leibstandarte; Das Reich would remain with

116

115
The Leibstandarte was transferred to Italy to boost the morale of the Italian troops still loyal to Mussolini.

116
A Leibstandarte Panzer IV in Milan. (Associated Press)

89

Army Group South. Furthermore the Leibstandarte would move without its tanks and heavy equipment, which would be handed over to other formations to bolster their combat worthiness.

A number of plans providing for the occupation of Rome and the rescue of Mussolini were conceived, but no precipitate action was taken until September when two events set the plans in operation. On 3 September Allied troops landed in southern Italy and five days later it was announced that Italy and the Allies had signed an armistice.

The plan to rescue Mussolini was code-named Operation *'Eiche'* ('Oak') and the problem with it was determining the location of the Duce's captivity. At the beginning of August it was reported that he had been spotted on the island of Ventotene, but by the middle of the month there were other reports that the Duce was being held on another island Maddalena, near the southern tip of

Sardinia. Elaborate arrangements were made to descend on the island with destroyers and paratroops, but before they could be carried out Mussolini had again been moved. According to a secret clause in the armistice agreement he was to be turned over to the Allies, but Badoglio delayed doing so and early in September the Duce was spirited away to a hotel on top of the 9,000ft high Gran Sasso d'Italia, the highest range in the Abruzzi Apeninnes, which could be reached only by a funicular railway.

The Germans soon learned of his whereabouts, made an aerial reconnaissance of the mountaintop and decided that glider-borne troops could probably land there, overcome the guards, and spirit the Duce away in a little Fieseler Storch aircraft. Accordingly this daring plan was carried out by Otto Skorzeny, who was subsequently promoted to SS-Standartenführer in recognition of the exploit. After kidnapping an Italian general, whom he packed into his glider, Skorzeny landed his SS force about a hundred yards from the hotel. Most of the carabinieri guarding Mussolini fled and and those who did not do so were dissuaded by Skorzeny from making use of their weapons. Pushing the captive general in front of him, Skorzeny yelled, 'Do not fire on an Italian general'. From the window of his room in the hotel Mussolini also shouted, 'Don't shoot anybody'. And nobody did shoot.

Within minutes the Fascist leader was bundled into the Fieseler Storch and, after a perilous take-off, flown by Skorzeny to Rome and from there to Vienna in a Luftwaffe transport plane. At Hitler's insistence, Mussolini proclaimed a new Italian Social Republic but the Duce was a broken man with little stomach for reviving the Fascist regime in German-occupied Italy. He never returned to Rome but set himself up in an isolated spot in the extreme north — at Rocco delle Carninate near Gargnano on the shores of Lake Garda. There he was closely guarded by a detachment of the Leibstandarte. And it was to this lakeside resort that Sepp Dietrich escorted Mussolini's most notorious mistress, Clara Petacci.

Besides guarding Mussolini, the Leibstandarte found time to re-equip and reorganise; for the men of the division the Italian interlude was a very welcome break after Russia. During their stay one tank battalion was issued with 'Panther' tanks — the very latest German armour.

117
SS-Obergruppenführer Karl Wolff with Benito Mussolini. Towards the end of the war Wolff (then an SS-Oberstgeneral) made contact with British intermediaries in Switzerland and tried to negotiate an armistice on the Italo-Austrian front. His efforts were sabotaged by Kesselring.

117

7
Normandy

When the Allies landed in Normandy in June 1944 there were five Waffen-SS divisions in France. Four of them — Das Reich, Hohenstaufen, Frundsberg and Hitlerjugend — were immediately committed to the battle to drive the invaders back into the sea; two months later they were joined by the Leibstandarte which had been resting and refitting after the severe mauling it had recently received in Russia.

The Hitlerjugend had only begun to train as a division in January 1944 but in April it moved to the Evreux-Bernay-Vimoutiers area west of Paris and south of Rouen. An Allied invasion of Europe had been on Hitler's mind for some time and the Hitlerjugend was positioned in this area in case the Allies landed on the Normandy coast. In May the division redeployed in the area between Trun and Chambois about six miles north-east of Argentan — the area where less than two months later it was to be virtually wiped out. The threat of an invasion was a real one but life for most of the troops deployed in defence of the 'Western Wall' was reasonably pleasant — so much so that SS Oberführer Fritz Witt, the divisional commander was moved to say: 'War could be so enjoyable if there wasn't always the possibility of getting killed!' (Witt himself was killed in fighting when the Hitlerjugend tried to smash the beachheads established by the British 7th and 50th Divisions.)

On the morning of Tuesday 6 June the Hitlerjugend and the Panzer-Lehr Divisions were ordered to engage the Allies on the Normandy beaches and to drive them back into the sea before the day was out. The Hitlerjugend with Fritz Witt in command was on the march by 1630 and it was the first Waffen-SS division to go into action in Normandy when it reached the outskirts of Caen. It was in the early hours of 7 June that the first SS Battle Group, consisting of 90 Panzer IVs and three battalions of fanatical young SS infantrymen under command of

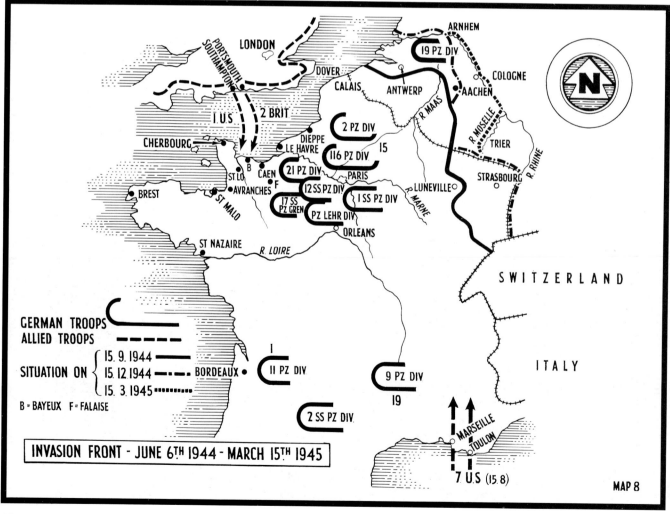

GERMAN TROOPS
ALLIED TROOPS ------

SITUATION ON ⎰ 15. 9. 1944 ———
             ⎱ 15. 12. 1944 —·—·
               15. 3. 1945 ·······

B = BAYEUX F = FALAISE

INVASION FRONT - JUNE 6TH 1944 - MARCH 15TH 1945

MAP 8

Standartenführer Kurt Meyer, engaged the tanks of the advancing 27th Canadian Armoured Regiment. A bloody battle developed and although Meyer's force was compelled to break off the attack the Canadians were unable to secure the Carpiquet airfield which the Allies would promptly have converted into a forward air base. This in turn postponed the fall of Caen.

Next day, 8 June, Meyer attacked again, without success. It was on this day that he is believed to have been responsible for the murder of 45 Canadian prisoners of war at Authie. This was but one of a series of atrocities when SS men of the Hitlerjugend shot unarmed prisoners-of-war after their interrogation. Between 7 June and 16 June, 64 Canadian and British prisoners are said to have been killed, and it was rumoured at the time that a divisional order stipulated that this was how prisoners were to be disposed of. After the war Meyer was tried by a Canadian court, found guilty and condemned to death. (In the event his sentence was commuted to life imprisonment and Meyer was released in September 1954.) No evidence of any written order to this effect has ever been forthcoming and it is probable that the atrocities were committed by fanatical young SS men, acting without official approval or sanction but whose actions were condoned by officers and NCOs in the immediate vicinity.

Between 13 and 15 June the Hitlerjugend, the 21st Armoured and Panzer-Lehr Divisions were preparing for an all-out assault on the British bridgehead when the British 49th Division launched an attack on their concentration area. This attack was supported by the heavy guns of a British battleship and cruisers standing offshore and some of this fire fell on the SS Division's headquarters, 17 miles south-west of Caen, killing Fritz Witt, the commander. The redoubtable Kurt Meyer took over and under his command Hitlerjugend stemmed for a few days an offensive by the British Second Army on the River Odon. But sheer weight of numbers and firepower brought an Allied break-through on 27 June and although the SS men launched a determined counter-attack it was repulsed with heavy losses.

118
British airborne troops and Waffen-SS PoWs, Arnhem 1944. (Imperial War Museum)

On 4 July the division came under attack again — this time from the Canadians, attempting yet again to seize the important airfield at Carpiquet. The initial attack was held but the men of the Hitlerjugend could take only so much, and when the British 3rd and 59th Divisions threw in their weight Caen fell. The little town which the SS men had held for 33 days was now little more than a heap of rubble and the division had lost 60% of its strength in casualties — one in three of these casualties being killed. Furthermore the remnants of the division had only half its tanks and armoured personnel carriers. So on 11 July the survivors of the Hitlerjugend were pulled back to the Potigny area for a rest and to give the division an opportunity to refit.

Both the rest and the refit had to be curtailed. On 18 July the British launched a new offensive east of Caen and the Hitlerjugend was rushed to the front with orders to stop the Allies breaking through between Maltot and Vendes. But a week after the British offensive was launched the Americans also attacked. Starting from St Lô they planned to crunch through the German front in Brittany and push on to the very heart of France. This was followed on 30 July by another British offensive. The outcome was that the Americans effected a breakthrough

at Avranches, and gained the base of the Cotentin — the region south of Cherbourg where another of the Waffen-SS Divisions, Das Reich, had successfully pinned down the US First Army. This opened up a gap through which the Allied armour whirled — one column swinging west into Brittany while another swung east towards the River Seine and Paris.

At this crucial stage of the battle the Hitlerjugend and the Leibstandarte (together forming the Ist SS-Panzer Corps) were holding a line running from the Falaise plateau towards Caen. To the utter astonishment of Sepp Dietrich, the corps commander, Hitler suddenly decided to step into the fray with an order that the two SS armoured divisions should go on the offensive and recapture Avranches. The Führer, far from the front and reality, had not grasped that the battle for Normandy was as good as lost; he was still thinking of an offensive which would bring final victory. Dietrich, on the other hand, appreciated that moving his two SS tank divisions from their defensive positions south of Caen would leave Falaise open to attack by the enemy. But objecting to a 'Führer order' was futile, and Dietrich directed his old division, the Leibstandarte to make the attempt to recapture Avranches while the Hitlerjugend

119
Canadians guard prisoners of the Hitlerjugend Division, Normandy 1944. (Public Archives of Canada)

119

stayed on in front of Falaise. Thus, on 6 August the Leibstandarte advanced westwards at Mortain towards Avranches, hoping after its capture to turn north and crush the Normandy beachheads. The Allies responded by shifting reinforcements and — with the aid of air power, mostly British — the German attack was halted on 8 August. The men of the Leibstandarte were almost exhausted but Hitler ordered the effort to continue for two more days. Meanwhile, oblivious to this threat, the Americans from the south-west and the British from the north bore down in the direction of Falaise in a pincer movement. The two Wehrmacht infantry divisions on the flanks of the Hitlerjugend rapidly disintegrated and the Hitlerjugend bore the brunt of the Allied onslaught. For a while the division managed to stand fast, but as casualties in men and machines mounted even the fanatics of the Hitlerjugend began to weaken under the pressure. By the evening of 8 August the division had only 48 tanks left out of the 218 with which they had gone into battle.

Following a massive air strike on the defences held by the shattered division, the 4th Canadian Armoured, 3rd Canadian Infantry and 1st Polish Armoured Divisions were sent in to finish off the Hitlerjugend. But Kurt Meyer had anticipated the air strike and

120

120
'Sepp' Dietrich congratulates SS-Obersturmbannführer Wilhelm Mohnke and officers of the Hitlerjugend Division, Normandy 1944.

121
Reich Youth Leader Axmann meets officers of the Hitlerjugend Division, Normandy 1944.

121

95

had moved the remnants of his division together with their few remaining vehicles away from their positions before the bombing began. Then as the Canadians and Poles mounted their attack, Meyer assembled his force in two battle groups and struck back, taking Clintheaux and checking the advance of the 4th Canadian Armoured Division. But this was a mere flash in the pan. After a brief pause the Canadians renewed their attack and recaptured Clintheaux while the Poles attempted to mop up the survivors of the Hitlerjugend. 30-year old SS-Obersturmbannführer Max Wünsche, the commander of the Division's armoured regiment (Panzer Regiment 12) who had recently been decorated with the Oak leaves to the Knight's Cross of the Iron Cross was severely wounded in this action and captured.

By 14 August the strength of the division had been reduced to only about 500 infantrymen, and these — under the direct command of Kurt Meyer — were holding Hill 159 north-east of Falaise. Meyer reported that the morale of his men was 'very high' despite the 48 hours heavy and continuous artillery bombardment and air strikes to which they were subjected prior to an attack by the 3rd Canadian Division.

However when the attack went in the SS-men were compelled to abandon Hill 159 and fall back to a new defensive position on the River Ante. Meyer himself was wounded in this action.

Falaise fell to the Allies on 16 August but a stubborn group of about 60 Hitlerjugend fanatics continued to hold out in a school long after the rest of the town had been overrun. When the shooting eventually stopped in Falaise only four of them — all wounded — were taken prisoner. Apart from two who had slipped away through the British lines and rejoined the remnants of their division which had meanwhile retreated to the southwest, the rest of the group had all been killed.

Allied misunderstandings and some timidity contributed to provide a gap at Falaise through which the much disorganised survivors of Paul Hausser's Seventh Army and the Fifth Panzer Army (of which Dietrich's Leibstandarte and Hitlerjugend were a part) could flee eastwards. The jaws of the Allies' pincers were closing rapidly and the Germans realised that it was still possible to extricate a large number of the troops deployed on the Normandy front if they operated quickly. So the Hitlerjugend and other armoured divisions were told to keep the jaws of the pincers open and the escape

122
Infantrymen of the Götz von Berlichingen Division (the 17th SS Panzergrenadier Division) Normandy 1944.

123
The Hitlerjugend Division gained a reputation for ruthlessness in Normandy, and any of its members who fell into Canadian hands were either shot or, if lucky, beaten up.

124

125

route clear as long as possible. Kurt Meyer's task was to hold the northern flank until General Eugen Meindl's 2nd Parachute Corps could break out of the Falaise 'Pocket' and to stop the Canadians reaching Chambois. Then Meyer was to follow Meindl across the Dives River, extricating as many of his Hitlerjugend men as he could.

To comply with this order an SS battle group was formed by amalgamating the combat-worthy elements of the division. This Kampfgruppe, under command of SS-Obersturmbannführer Wilhelm Mohnke, the commander of the Hitlerjugend's second infantry regiment, succeeded in escorting most of the remaining units of the Division out of the Falaise trap to safety across the Seine.

Throughout the battle for Normandy the other four Waffen-SS divisions in France had been in the thick of the fighting. Das Reich was in the south of the country when the Allies launched their invasion and as they motored north to Normandy the division passed through the village of Oradour-sur-Glane. As they did so a Maquis sniper shot and killed one of the division's officers. In a ruthless reprisal the SS destroyed every house and shot most of the population, noting in the divisional war diary that the

village was destroyed after 'munitions' were discovered in almost every house.

In Normandy Das Reich, deployed in the St Lô area, attempted to contain the invaders on the beaches. However on 3 July the American First Army initiated the offensive that became known as the battle of the 'Hedgerows'. The 'hedgerows' are walls, half earth and half hedge enclosing the tiny fields in the Cotentin, the region south of Cherbourg. Confined in a relatively small sector and confronted with difficult terrain and inadequate roads, the Americans fought a determined enemy favoured by these endless lines of natural fortifications (the hedgerows) and assisted by incessant rain which denied Allied tactical air support, and reduced observation. In the event the Germans — mostly SS men of Das Reich — inflicted some 40,000 casualties on the US First Army before the Americans effected the breakthrough at Avranches and gained the Cotentin. The Das Reich tried to seal the gap created by the Americans but having failed to do so it was compelled to fall back or run the risk of being cut off. At this point in time it looked as if all five SS divisions together with six Wehrmacht armoured divisions and eight infantry divisions would be trapped in the Falaise-Argentan pocket unless the jaws

124, 125
SS armour moves up in Normandy, June 1944: A Panzer IV (124) and Sturmgeshütz IIIs. (Bibliotheque Nationale)

126
'Sepp' Dietrich shows a Wehrmacht general some of the new equipment received by the Leibstandarte in Normandy in 1944. 'Panzer' Meyer is on the general's left.

127

This dead SS man was a sniper who was ordered to stay behind in Falaise when the main German forces withdrew from the town. (Canadian Army Photograph)

of the Allied pincers could be kept open. The part played by the Hitlerjugend in holding off one arm of the pincer has been described. The other arm was held back by the Hohenstaufen, but at considerable cost. Nevertheless both divisions, severely mauled but still intact, managed to escape before the jaws of the trap snapped shut.

The Hohenstaufen's sister division, the Frundsberg, was not so fortunate. It had already sustained heavy losses at Caen and Avranches when it was trapped in the 'pocket' and virtually annihilated; only a few men managed to escape and make their way north and across the Seine.

Towards the end of June the Leibstandarte was flung into the battle for Normandy. This division had been resting, recuperating and refitting near Bruges in Belgium after the drubbing it had taken in Russia during February. But in April it had become part of the High Command's strategic reserve and so under Hitler's direct control. As soon as the Führer realised that the Allied invasion force was not going to be defeated on the beaches his 'bodyguard' division was com-

mitted. Nearing the Normandy battlefield the Leibstandarte's vehicles were spotted by Allied aircraft and subjected to repeated attacks by fighter-bombers, and then had to run a gauntlet through heavy concentrations of artillery fire. Around Caen the division faced the Canadian 3rd Division and there was some bitter fighting in the Normandy countryside as the SS men, with years of combat experience, battled with determined troops most of whom had been campaigning barely a month.

After heavy engagements at Caen, Falaise and Argentan the remnants of the Leibstandarte made their way back to the Siegfried Line. There, some of the survivors were mustered into a composite unit 'SS-Bataillon Rink' (so-called after its commander) and — together with 'SS-Bataillon Bucher' formed from some of the survivors of the Hitlerjugend — became part of Kampfgruppe Diesenthal. This battle group was responsible for the defence of Aachen.

The remaining Hitlerjugend survivors who had escaped when the jaws of the Allied

pincers finally closed near Chambois on 20 August regrouped on the nucleus of their own battle group — SS Kampfgruppe Mohnke. There were no vehicles to bother about and only about 600 men; these were sent to Kaiserslautern. Only a few days were spent refitting before the newly constituted and much reduced Hitlerjugend Division was off to the front again — in time for the retreat through France to the Franco-Belgian border. On 3 September it reached Philippeville and the following day the River Meuse; two days after that the divisional commander, Kurt Meyer, was captured near Amiens.

After their escape from the Falaise Pocket the remnants of Das Reich and Hohenstaufen retreated across the lower Seine near Rouen and across France to the German frontier. Both divisions had been badly battered, having fought continuously with diminishing strength as no replacements were forthcoming during the Normandy battles. In July the Hohenstaufen had even lost its divisional commander, SS-Oberführer Sylvester Stadler, who was wounded and

128
SS NCO is captured and searched by Americans in Normandy. (Imperial War Museum)

129
SS-Sturmbannführer Fritz Witt, commander of the 1st Battalion of the SS-Regiment Deutschland of the SS-Verfügungs Division and later commander of the Hitlerjugend Division.

evacuated to hospital. However once the survivors had crossed the Dutch border and arrived at Veluwe, north of Arnhem, it seemed as if they were to enjoy a break. On 10 September — three days after their arrival — an order was issued to the effect that the men of the division (now only about 2,500 of them instead of the established strength of 12,500) were to hand over their tanks and weapons to the Frundsberg which would reform in Holland.

On 17 September the SS men were on the point of entraining for Germany when the Allies launched Operation 'Market Garden' and the British 1st Airborne Division landed on the outskirts of Arnhem and near Nijmegen. The drops took the unsuspecting Germans completely by surprise. Field Marshal Walther Model, the German commander-in-chief in Holland, thought that airborne commandos had been sent to kidnap him and he hurried to take refuge at the headquarters of SS-Obergruppenführer 'Willi' Bittrich, commander of II SS-Panzer Corps composed of the Hohenstaufen and Frundsberg divisions. Bittrich had a hunch that something much bigger than the kidnapping of a field marshal was afoot and he ordered everybody to stand to. Under his orders also a battle group was hastily formed from the remnants of the Hohenstaufen.

(This in itself was no easy problem as the serviceable vehicles were supposed to have been handed over to the Frundsberg.) This battle group — 'Kampfgruppe Hartzer' — was handled with skill and efficiency by its commander SS-Standartenführer Walter Harzer, who was subsequently awarded the Knights' Cross of the Iron Cross. Nevertheless it took four days of fierce fighting before the lightly-armed British paratroops were overwhelmed. Many British soldiers fell into the hands of the Waffen-SS and they were astonished by and decidely wary of the attitude of their SS captors who jovially handed out cigarettes, chocolate and brandy. (Bitterly the paratroops recognised the cigarettes and chocolate as British-made and thus in all probability part of the air supplies that had been intended for them anyway.) Bittrich himself said later that it was 'a matter of chivalry' to show due respect to his adversaries in the Arnhem-Nijmegen fighting. 'These men', he said, 'were tough, well-trained soldiers — typically British — who we had been fighting since D-Day. Their morale was superb. The troops at the Arnhem bridge fought a hard and gallant battle, and at the end of it their morale was still high'. [He also told the author (in 1978) that he had never been so sickened by the sight of carnage as he was sickened at Arnhem.]

130
SS-Brigadeführer Heinz Harmel, commander of the 10th SS-Panzer Division Frundsberg in Normandy, 1944. It was Harmel who commanded Frundberg at Arhem.

8

The Battle of the Bulge

At the beginning of November 1944 what remained of the Leibstandarte, Das Reich, Hohenstaufen and Hitlerjugend Divisions were pulled back to western Germany to be reorganised, refitted and rehabilitated prior to their being incorporated into the Sixth Panzer Army under Sepp Dietrich (recently promoted to SS-Oberstgruppenführer and Generaloberst der Waffen-SS). This Sixth Panzer Army was composed of two corps — the Ist and IInd SS Panzer Corps; the Leibstandarte and the Hitlerjugend Divisions constituted the Ist Corps, Das Reich and the Hohenstaufen made up the IInd. Dietrich's newly constituted force was one of three armoured armies which were committed to the massive and daring offensive in the Ardennes — now better known as the Battle of the Bulge — that Hitler intended should change the whole course of the war. The strategic and political aims of this offensive were to divide the British and American armies, capture their main source of supplies and frustrate Britain's ability to continue the war in Europe. Even if this latter objective were not achieved the war would definitely be extended and the Führer confidently expected that the Anglo-American-Soviet coalition would then break down.

The plan was for a German armoured force to break through the thinly held American line between Rötgen and Losheim and rip through to Antwerp, and it was hoped that all the Allied forces north of the line Antwerp-Brussels-Bastogne would be destroyed, just as in 1940. Success depended on three elements — effecting a breakthrough, seizing Allied fuel supplies and key focal points of communication in the St Vith and Bastogne regions and finally of widening the gap where the initial break-through had been made. In the event the task of effecting the initial break-through was given to the Ist SS-Panzer Corps and its spearhead was a strong battle group of Leibstandarte. This battle group — Kampfgruppe Peiper, commanded by the tough and able Jochen Peiper — comprised some 5,000 men equipped with Tiger, Panther and Royal Tiger tanks, self-propelled guns, mobile AA units, engineers and a battalion of Panzergrenadiers.

The offensive was launched on 16 December 1944, after a period of fog, rain and snow which had blanketed Allied aerial observation and hobbled combat capabilities. Complete strategic surprise was achieved and Peiper's Kampfgruppe quickly smashed through the American line at Losheim and

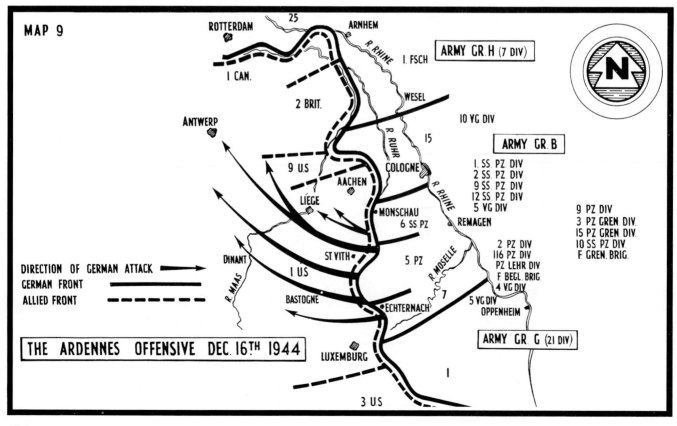

headed west for Baugnez and Malmedy. The route, Peiper complained to his divisional commander Mohnke, was 'more suited to bicycles than tanks'. Nevertheless, although the terrain slowed the progress of his 72ton Royal Tigers, by the morning of 18 December his forward units had covered more than 20 miles from Losheim. The advance had been less spectacular in other sectors but about 50 German columns were now probing into the Ardennes from Monschau in the north and Echternach in the south. American resistance had stiffened in some areas and the Hitlerjugend Division had run into stiff opposition near Bütgenbach some seven miles east of Malmedy. There it was to have linked up with the Leibstandarte's Kampfgruppe but when the US 1st Infantry Division arrived on the scene and counter-attacked at Bütgenbach it was decided that it would be quicker to break off the action there, swing the division round, and follow the route taken by the Leibstandarte. Meanwhile further south the Hohenstaufen and the Das Reich were fighting in the dense forests between Malmedy and St Vith.

Malmedy was a focal point in the Battle of the Bulge but the name of this village was to become better known as the result of the massacre of 71 unarmed American prisoners of war at the Malmedy cross-roads by

131

132

131, 132
Waffen-SS troops during the Ardennes Offensive. Two from a series of photographs posed in front of a knocked out American M8 Greyhound armoured car. (Imperial War Museum and US Army photographs)

133
Another well-known Ardennes campaign photograph. This is one of a sequence of photographs shot on the road from St Vith to Malmedy and purports to show Jochen Peiper. Recent opinion tends to disagree with this.

134
Waffen-SS troops during the Ardennes Offensive. (Imperial War Museum and US Army photographs)

135
Waffen-SS prisoners of the 50th Armoured Infantry Regiment, 7 January 1945.

136
An SS-War correspondent-photographer.

members of Kampfgruppe Peiper. Both Sepp Dietrich and Peiper were deemed to be responsible for this activity — Peiper because he was alleged to have issued an order on the 'disposal' of prisoners of war on the line of march, and Dietrich who, as army commander, had condoned the order. Peiper was sentenced to death in February 1946 but freed 10 years later because American officers had used irregular methods of interrogation before the trial. Dietrich who was sentenced to 25 years imprisonment, also had his sentence remitted and was set free.

On the northern flank of the German offensive the American Vth Corps held firm; so too did the US 4th Division on the south. Canalised between these two shoulders, however, the attack raced on towards the Meuse. By Christmas Eve Das Reich was within three miles of the river. But the Allies rushed up reinforcements — two US armoured divisions and the US 82nd and 101st Airborne Divisions — and although the Hohenstaufen forged ahead slowly around St Vith, the offensive had lost its momentum, and there was no hope of the Germans reaching Antwerp. Meantime by 19 December Kampfgruppe Peiper had been virtually cut off from its supplies and encircled — trapped in the Amblève river

valley near the villages of Stoumont, La Gleize and Cheneux. When Peiper was told that American troops had captured Stavelot and blown the bridge there he ordered an immediate assault to drive the 'Amis' out.

Six Tiger tanks and two companies of Peiper's reconnaissance battalion advanced towards the village in two columns. American artillery observation officers soon spotted the first column moving down a road which constituted a defile, with the river on the right and a steep hillside on the left. A hail of shells, fitted with a new type of artillery proximity fuze, rained down on the helplessly exposed Germans and within a matter of minutes the advance of the column had been halted. The American artillery was now directed on to the second column taking another route and which had succeeded in advancing almost as far as Stavelot, where some of the inhabitants — thinking the approaching vehicles were Americans — had run out to greet them. Again the deadly barrage descended and the advance of the second column came to an abrupt halt and a number of the civilians were killed in the bombardment. More were killed shortly afterwards when a group of wild young SS men went into some of the houses, slaughtered the inmates and set the houses on

fire — presumably to hide the crime. Four civilians were shot in the hamlet of Ster about this time and 15 outside it; at Renardmont 19 others were killed and at Hurlet Farm 12 people were mown down. The dead included a nine-month old baby and a 78-year old woman.

Survivors said that the murderers were young men barely out of their teens. No doubt they were frightened and frustrated, and their justification for the shootings was that the villagers were hiding Americans who had been responsible for the heavy casualties the attacking columns had incurred. There was more horror to come. Later that night other villagers were systematically 'executed' on the grounds that the people of Stavelot had been harbouring American soldiers. All-in-all 130 civilians were killed around Stavelot on 19 December 1944 — 47 women, 23 children and 60 men. Peiper himself was not directly involved in the killings but he did say to one of the villagers who appealed for him for help when the SS men were going from house to house searching for Americans: 'All you people in this region are terrorists.'

The armoured attack on Stavelot having failed, Peiper ordered the Panzergrenadiers to wade across the icy cold Amblève during the early hours of 20 December. As they crossed another thunderous barrage of fire rained down on the SS men and their advance wavered and broke. Silhouetted against the light of burning houses and flares the Panzergrenadiers were easy targets for the American riflemen. Showing incredible courage Peiper's men reformed and tried again. Most of this second wave were mown down in the river, like their predecessors. However a few men did succeed in getting a foothold on the American-held river-bank but their tiny bridgehead was quickly wiped out.

Later in the day the Americans set out to destroy Peiper's Kampfgruppe and armoured fighting vehicles of the US 740th Tank Battalion advanced under cover of the thick fog which shrouded the Stoumont-La Gleize area. Peiper's vehicles, lacking petrol, were immobilised. But his tanks were by no means impotent and the Americans were severely mauled. US infantry managed to battle their way into Stoumont but Peiper launched a counter-attack and there was some savage hand-to-hand fighting before the SS were eventually forced to withdraw.

At Cheneux, south of Stoumont, men of the US 82nd Airborne Division stormed across 400 yards of open ground to attack the German positions. Three times they tried, and three times they failed to reach the wire which the SS had hurriedly thrown round their trenches — cut down by the waist-high fire of light AA guns. But on their fourth attempt they succeeded in reaching and penetrating the German line. Once established there they began systematically to stalk and destroy the AA guns which had caused them so many casualties. Blood was up on both sides and neither gave nor asked for quarter.

By 21 December Peiper's Kampfgruppe had been completely surrounded and he was virtually immobilised by lack of fuel. Although SS Oberführer Mohnke, his divisional commander, assured him over the radio that the Kampfgruppe would be relieved, Peiper realised that from his point of view the military situation was deteriorating. So, during the late afternoon the men of the Kampfgruppe that were still able to fight began to concentrate in the hilltop village of La Gleize; those who were too badly wounded to walk were left behind for the Americans to tend.

At this stage it was clear that the Ardennes offensive was going badly and Sepp Dietrich himself appreciated that there could be no question of capturing Hitler's ultimate objective — Antwerp. Indeed Dietrich had never believed that his undersupplied Sixth Army could ever capture the port. But he had believed in the intermediate objective — the crossing of the Meuse — and he had set his hopes on the Peiper Kampfgruppe seizing the Meuse bridge. Now it was apparent that Peiper was in dire trouble, from which he could be extracted only if the rest of the Leibstandarte could break through to its isolated Kampfgruppe. In the event Mohnke's men could not break through; meanwhile Peiper's situation was deteriorating rapidly. The village of La Gleize in which the survivors of his Kampfgruppe had concentrated was now rocked by continual artillery bombardment; the Americans had already infiltrated one end of the village. Over the radio came nothing but irritating bureaucratic demands for information. (After the war, when he was asked what he would do if he were to conduct the Ardennes operation again, Peiper said that he would, 'Put a general at each street corner to regulate traffic'.) Eventually Peiper could take no more. Over the radio in the middle of the bombardment he asked to speak to the divisional commander and Mohnke responded. 'Almost all our "Hermann" (Ammunition) is gone and we have no "Otto" (fuel). It's a matter of time before we are annihilated. May we have permission to break out.' There was silence for a while and then the Leibstandarte divisional commander asked, 'Can you break out with all vehicles and wounded?'. Peiper replied, '*Without* wounded and vehicles . . . it's our last chance tonight.' Mohnke said he could not give permission but he would talk to the Corps Commander, Generalleutnant der Waffen-SS Hermann Preiss and he, presumably, would have to talk to Sepp Dietrich the Army Commander.

Peiper put down the microphone and switched off. Turning to his radio officer he said: 'Permission or not we're breaking out of here on foot.' That night between two and three in the morning on Sunday 24 December the surviving SS men of the Kampfgruppe slipped out of La Gleize and made their way in little groups down the slope which led to the Amblève river. There were only about 800 left of the 5,000 who had set out a week before. A few volunteers had stayed behind to destroy the vehicles and heavy equipment they had abandoned in the village and at about 0400 hours the night was shattered by a series of deafening explosions and the tanks went up in flames. Having done their job the volunteers raced down the slope towards the river to join the rest of the survivors of Kampfgruppe Peiper. Most of them managed to swim across the river in the early hours of Christmas morning and they were welcomed back like victors by other Leibstandarte men on the south bank. A day later they were sent to the rear to recuperate and to be re-equipped. But the decimated 1st SS-Panzer Regiment, the backbone of the Kampfgruppe, was not to fight again in the Ardennes battle.

The Battle of the Bulge was not over in fact, although it was now clear that Hitler's gamble had failed. The Hohenstaufen and Das Reich divisions were still fighting in the dense forest around St Vith and St Vith had fallen to the Germans only when two infantry divisions of the LXVIth Corps attacked from the east and the Hohenstaufen and Führer Escort-Brigade (*Führerbegleitbrigade*) from the north. In the course of the fighting which followed a large portion of Das Reich was cut off and an entire regiment destroyed.

With the offensive grinding to a halt close to the Meuse, Hitler insisted that Bastogne should be captured, and for a week while the German tide ebbed elsewhere in the Bulge under Allied pressure a furious battle raged around the town. On 6 January 1945 the Ist SS-Panzer Corps launched what was to be the last of the major attacks on Bastogne. When this was repulsed Hitler realised that it was hopeless continuing with the Ardennes offensive, and the Sixth Panzer Army was withdrawn. When the battered SS formations pulled out the Bulge was gradually eliminated and by 18 January the German armies had returned to the positions they were holding before the offensive began.

Meantime Hitler was planning yet another desperate offensive — this time on the eastern front where the situation was becoming critical.

137
Highly decorated wounded members of the Waffen-SS on leave in Germany and in conversation with female tram conductress.

137

9
The Last Act

In June 1944 the Russians launched another great offensive in step with the Anglo-American invasion of France. Minsk was captured on 3 July, some 25 German divisions were trapped, and the Russians subsequently claimed they had taken 158,000 prisoners and killed 381,000 other Germans. Only a week later yet another Russian offensive led to the Finnish defences being overrun and in September hostilities between Finland and Russia ceased. Meantime other Soviet armies had been driving into Poland, advancing on Warsaw and penetrating on the northern flank towards Riga. By July the Russians were fighting in the suburbs of the Polish capital and the situation was stabilised only when the newly formed IVth SS-Panzer Corps composed of the SS-Panzer Divisions Wiking and Totenkopf counter-attacked and drove the Russians out of the city and back across the Vistula. It was during this period while the Russians were on their very doorstep that the Polish underground forces in Warsaw rose in revolt and attempted to wrest the city from German control — hoping that the Russians would help them. But the Russians lay idle, while the SS men crushed the revolt in a bloody two-month house-to-house battle.

The situation on this northern sector of the Eastern front remained relatively quiet until January 1945. But to the south the Russians launched yet another great offensive across the Prut River and Rumania capitulated on 23 August. The Russians continued their advance and reached the Danube at Bucharest on 1 September where the SS-Cavalry Division Florian Geyer and the SS-Freiwilligen Cavalry Division were among the 50,000 German troops trapped in the city. The encircled garrison managed to keep the Russians at bay for a time and, on Christmas Eve 1944, Hitler ordered the Totenkopf and Wiking Divisions to abandon the defence of Warsaw and to 'raise the siege of Budapest'. The relief forces launched their attack on New Year's Day 1945; 10 days later they had battled their way through to Budapest airport. At that time the rescue of the encircled garrison seemed assured; four days later however the picture looked very different. Russian resistance had stiffened and the garrison was exhausted. In the event the fighting was called off at the end of January and the garrison surrendered on

12 February. Before the surrender, however, about 800 of the garrison managed to break out and fight their way through the Russian lines to reach the relief force. Among them were 170 men of the Waffen-SS — the sole survivors of the Florian Geyer Division — whose commander, the young and newly promoted SS-Brigadeführer Joachim Rumohr, committed suicide when he was wounded during the escape. That was the end of the Florian Geyer for the survivors were grouped together with other stragglers to form an SS cavalry group (the nucleus of the 37th SS Cavalry Division Lützow).

Following the fall of Bucharest the Totenkopf and Wiking Divisions dug in near Stuhlweissenburg, west of Budapest, and tried to hold up the steam-roller advance of the Soviet armies. It was a futile effort; heavy fighting resulted in severe casualties and the Wiking Division was virtually annihilated. The survivors and the remnants of the Totenkopf Division then retreated to Vienna where there was more intense fighting before the Russians captured the city. So far as the men of these two divisions were concerned, no doubt they thought the last act had been played out when they surrendered to the Americans on 9 May. But their luck was out; four days later the Americans handed them over to the Russians.

Sepp Dietrich's reformed Sixth Panzer Army was also thrown into the fighting around Budapest in March. Hitler was so concerned with sealing the gap that had been ripped in the German lines when the Russians initiated their winter offensive that reinforcements were fed forward as if into a mincing machine. Without any artillery preparation or air cover the SS units motored straight to their doom and within a week they were fighting a rearguard action as they fell back into Austria. Dietrich was ordered to regroup and stand before Vienna; Vienna was to be defended to the proverbial last man and last round and under no circumstances were the SS to withdraw into the city itself. In effect the SS men had little choice. Sixty Soviet divisions hammered them back, and they sought refuge in the built-up area. In doing so they lost touch with the Wehrmacht troops of General Hermann Balck's 6th Army on the right flank and an angry Balck said to General Otto Wöhler commander of Army Group South 'If the Leibstandarte

138
SS troops in action in Warsaw during the revolt, September 1944.

139
SS-Obergruppenführer Eric von dem Back Zelewski, commander of the 10th SS Army Corps, greets General Bor-Komorowski as he arrives at German headquarters to negotiate the surrender of the Polish Home Army. (Imperial War Museum)

140
German and Finnish officers at the Russian front in the far northern sector.

110

138

139

140

can't hold their ground, what do you expect us to do?' This remark, typical of Wehrmacht-SS rivalry, found its way back to Hitler. The latter was furious and sent the following message to Dietrich: 'The Führer believes that the troops have not fought as the situation demanded and orders that the SS Divisions Adolf Hitler (Leibstandarte), Das Reich, Totenkopf and Hohenstaufen be stripped of their cuffbands.' Colonel-General Heinz Guderian, the Wehrmacht Chief of Staff, was ordered to go to the crumbling southern front and see to it personally that the order was obeyed. Guderian refused, reminding Hitler that Reichsführer-SS Himmler was solely responsible for Waffen-SS disciplinary matters. Meantime in Vienna Dietrich summoned his divisional commanders to his headquarters and said: 'There's your reward for all that you've done these past five years.' He then ordered that not a single cuffband should be removed and sent a stiff message back to Hitler's headquarters. (The story is that he packed up his own decorations in a chamber pot and sent that off to Hitler too. Whether or not this is true, the story catches the spirit of Dietrich's feelings.)

The Hitlerjugend Division also formed part of Sepp Dietrich's Sixth Panzer Army and when the German offensive (incongruously code-named *Frühlingserwachen* — Awakening of spring) against the Soviet forces in Hungary opened, this division advanced up the northern shore of Lake Balaton. The plan was that there would be a two-pronged attack — one prong heading south towards Szenszard on the Sarviz Canal with the aim eventually of reaching the Danube. The other prong would reach the Danube at Dunapentele and then head north to retake Budapest. The advance of both forces soon lost momentum, however. Not only had the Germans to cope with stiffening Soviet resistance but the weather played into the Soviet hands. First there was freezing weather, followed by a thaw in February which made the roads heave. Then on the day before the SS men were scheduled to attack a blizzard made movement even more difficult. In the event the Hitlerjugend postponed the start until next day. And when the attack did eventually get under way the weather suddenly warmed up, thawing the frozen ground and turning it into a quagmire.

The SS men pressed on as best they could though without the verve of the tank attacks which had characterised most Waffen-SS operations. After six days of fighting the Hitlerjugend had gained only five miles and eventually by the middle of March the advance ground to a halt and a determined

141

112

Soviet counter-offensive forced a withdrawal.

The battered Hitlerjugend retreated northwest back into Austria. Vienna, where units of Das Reich had tried to stem the Russian advance by holding the vital Danube Canal bridge in the heart of the city, surrendered on 13 April. Realising that the final act was now being played out, Sepp Dietrich's prime concern now was to save his SS divisions from the Russians. Most of these divisions were scattered and partially disorganised; moreover morale was sagging. (The Der Führer Regiment of Das Reich, for example, was trying to put down a revolt in Prague early in May, while other units of the division were heavily engaged west of Vienna and others were also in action east of Dresden.)

As the Russians advanced deeper into Austria the Hitlerjugend Division and elements of the Leibstandarte withdrew past Odenburg and Hirtenburg, to a defensive position in the mountainous Wienerwald area south-west of Vienna. But after only a few days the SS men pulled out and resumed their retreat, moving west towards Linz and the Americans. Even the most fanatical members of the Division realised that the war was all but over and both officers and men preferred to fall into American rather than Russian hands. On 8 May the division crossed the zonal boundary near the town of Enns near Linz and surrendered to the Americans. Proud and stubborn to the very end they had refused to comply with an American order that their vehicles should be draped with white flags as a token of surrender. Before crossing into the American occupied zone and less than a mile from the zonal boundary the remnants of the division, 455 men and one solitary tank paraded and were inspected by the divisional commander SS-Brigadeführer and General der Waffen-SS Hugo Kraas. Then they piled arms and marched into captivity.

Among the other Waffen-SS formations deserving mention in regard to the closing stages of the war is the SS-Freiwilligen-Gebirgs Division of Prinz Eugen. (This was a Waffen-SS division, manned by ethnic Germans from Serbia and Croatia, and created for anti-partisan warfare in Yugoslavia.) From the time it took the field in October 1942 the division was engaged in putting down partisans almost without interruption until the end of the war. The survivors of the division surrendered near Cilli, a town in Slovenia in May 1945 and were held as prisoners of war in Yugoslavia. Many were charged with war crimes and the Yugoslav War Crimes Commission stated that the Prinz Eugen Division committed some of the worst atrocities attributable to

142

141
British troops conduct blindfolded SS officers through their lines to negotiate a surrender, Italy 7 May 1945. (Imperial War Museum)

142
A knocked-out half-track Sd Kfz 250 of the Nordland Division in one of the rubble-strewn streets in Berlin.

143

Waffen-SS PoWs in Khersee, Austria shortly after the German capitulation. These prisoners are parading for work. (US Army photograph)

any soldiers in World War 2. Partisan activities are an unothodox method of waging war, of course, and no doubt the SS men suffered considerable provocation. However there could be no excuse for the excesses they committed such as the number of prisoners, and the torture and massacre of helpless civilians.

At this stage of the war there was one last drama to played out: the Soviet attack on Berlin. By this time the war in the West was having disastrous impact on the battles being waged on the Eastern front. And it was clear

to the average soldier that the war was over. Thus the primary objective of the soldiers on the Eastern front — especially the Waffen-SS and particularly the foreign volunteers who came from the Baltic countries of Latvia, Lithuania and Estonia serving with the once formidable Nordland Division — was to fall into American or British hands; at all costs they did not wish to be captured by the Russians.

In January what was left of the Nordland Division had been withdrawn from the Eastern Front and redeployed in Pomerania

114

troops were no different from those of the Americans or the British, none of whom had the slightest intention of taking unnecessary risks now that all was over bar the shouting. Few of the war reports and reminiscences of the battle for Berlin give an accurate picture of the battle scene. The overall impression is one of Hitler Youth equipped with Panzerfausts roaming bullet-swept streets, Waffen-SS snipers potting at Red Army men from the upper floors of Berlin tenements and Soviet tanks firing back and burying the snipers beneath the debris — and, of course, the bombs and the artillery fire, destruction from a safe distance, carrying practically no risk.

Russian reports of the fighting are typified by the following which appeared in *Pravda*:
'After we had passed a score of hills, lakes and innumerable little streams and canals near Seelow, our men painted the slogan "First to fire on Berlin" on their gun barrels. Fighting was still going on near the township of Hirschfeld, when the voice of the divisional commander, Major of the Guards Demodiv, gave the order: "Fire on Berlin"! That was at 1310 hours on 21 April. Suddenly a number of strange apparitions loomed up, wearing civilian jackets but khaki trousers and jackboots. "Are you soldiers?" "No." The sour smell of cheap alcohol from their impudent, drunken faces assailed our nostrils. They were all snot-nosed brats of the Hitler Youth. One was gulping and crying. They had been firing on our units from ambush. Having been caught, they tried to change quickly into civvies and run away. Policemen in immaculate greatcoats crept out of other cellars. They saluted snappily and immediately betrayed the entire police command.'

The survivors of one Norland battle group attempted to hold the village of Eggersdorf and their annihilation was described in *Izvestia*:
'Well camouflaged, our reconnaissance troops approached the first houses of the locality under cover from the NW. By questioning the local population and by personal observation, the Lieutenant established that the place was crowded with Hitlerite infantry, but that there were no tanks. He decided to test the enemy strength in force, and accordingly sent his tanks in at full speed. The other units followed his example. The annihilation of the Hitlerite infantry began. The Fascists retreated, but

in another desperate attempt to stabilise the situation and halt the Russian drive towards the capital. In the face of vastly superior numbers this effort had no more success than previous ones, and the small isolated battle groups which was what the division had been reduced to were gradually forced back into Berlin. On 25 April the Nordland men were fighting around Tempelhof airfield and the Russians had occupied the eastern suburbs of the German capital.

But the Russians were moving with extraordinary caution. At this time their

were mown down by our tanks and light artillery. A number of Fascists guns opened desultory fire. Soon the last Fascist gun had been silenced by our tanks.'

This account loses much of its drama when it is realised that the total strength of the Nordland Kampfgruppe at the start of this battle was 70 men and three 7.5cm anti-tank guns.

Meantime at Hitler's Headquarters in the Reichskanzlei the realisation that Berlin was about to be overrun by the Russians was beginning to dawn. There was a contingency plan for the Nordland Division to break out of Berlin through the Grunewald, taking Hitler with them. But by mid-April the situation had become so grave that even the Führer had come to realise that the plan had little chance of success. All hopes of his escaping from the encircled Berlin were gone. In one of his fits of rage Hitler nominated the divisional commander, SS-Brigadeführer Joachim Ziegler as the scapegoat, relieved him of his command and confined him under arrest in the Führerbunker. In his place as commander of the Nordland Hitler appointed SS-Brigadeführer Dr Gustav Krukenberg, of the Charlemagne Division. In the event Krukenberg did no better than his predecessor, and his comments (in *Kampftage in Berlin*) on the situation in Berlin vis-

144
SS troops in the Battle of Vienna.

145
Marburg, Germany, March 1945. Waffen-SS men carry a wounded comrade into captivity. The vehicle is one belonging to the American Third Armoured Division. (Imperial War Museum)

145

a-vis its Waffen-SS defenders are interesting.

On 24 April Krukenberg was all set to move, with his staff, from Strelitz — some 60 miles north of the capital — down to Berlin when Himmler drove past in an open Mercedes:

'About 90 of my men were lined up on either side of the road ... and to my surprise the Reichsführer did not stop, even though this was his first chance of inspecting members of the Charlemagne Division, which had been formed the year before. (These men of the Charlemagne were mostly Frenchmen.)

'Later I discovered that Himmler had just met Bernadotte in Lübeck. As he knew all about our orders, and seeing that he had been trying to negotiate a surrender, he ought, in all conscience, to have stopped us from going on to Berlin or at least have informed me about the situation. I have no doubt that, by driving straight past us, Himmler was trying to avoid this painful necessity.'

In Berlin Krukenberg had some difficulty in locating the headquarters of the Nordland, where he was to take over from Ziegler. At the Führerbunker where he reported first he was told that the telephone contact with the Nordland had been lost, but that the headquarters was somewhere on the Hasenheide, an open piece of land between the suburbs of Kreuzberg and Neukölln. Following a hair-raising drive through the empty streets of Berlin Krukenberg eventually found the headquarters in a bombed out building:

'The garrison was on the ground floor. They had suffered heavy casualties, and wounded men were lying around everywhere. Among them, was the divisional commander, Ziegler, who had been expecting to be relieved of his command. When I asked him what forces he was deploying in the front line, he shocked me by quoting the figure of 70 men. The rest of his troops were completely exhausted. But they would soon recover ...

'The Hasenheide was now under light artillery fire. Small Nordland units were guarding it and the neighbouring terrain against possible surprise attacks. Farther to the front we had nothing but Volkssturm units. Armed with captured rifles, and short of ammunition, these men cut rather poor figures.

'While the Volkssturm commander and I were discussing the chances of improving our forward defences, two Soviet tanks drew up on the opposite side of the Hermannplatz and opened fire. As they were alone, I thought the chances of destroying them at close range were fairly good. I told the district leader that I would give the necessary orders and that I would take some of the burden off his men, as well. I returned safely to the Hasenheide, apart from a slight shrapnel wound in the face. My commando had meanwhile arrived from the Reich Sports Stadium ... I deployed half the French (volunteer) anti-tank group under Capt Fenet against the Soviet armour we had already sighted and against any other that might be expected ... During the evening and night, the French managed to shoot up 14 Soviet tanks at very close range, with the result that the enemy advance was temporarily stopped. Later on, too, it was repeatedly shown that the counter-action, even if only by a single machine gun sufficed to stop the Russians in their tracks.'

This was the beginning of the last fight by the handful of French Waffen-SS men who — first in Neukölln and later in the centre of Berlin — considerably upset the Russians by the courage and skill they showed in hunting down tanks. In the early hours of 28 April 1945 the Russians threw pontoon bridges across the Landwehr canal near the Halle Gate and soon afterwards sent over a large number of tanks. Krukenberg wrote:

'Since then fighting has been going on for every house, ruin and shell crater. Losses on both sides have been high. In our case, they were inflicted not only by enemy guns but also by the collapse of buildings under constant artillery bombardment. Nevertheless, on that day and the next the Nordland grenadiers succeeded in holding the position allocated to them, apart, that is, from a few local Soviet breaches which were quickly sealed up again. Our guns, and especially our French anti-tank units, played an important part in the defence. Eugene Vaulot, a French NCO, shot up six enemy tanks within 24 hours of destroying two T-34s in Neukölln. At my recommendation he was given the Knight's Cross, which I was privileged to bestow upon him during the afternoon of 29 April, in the presence of my staff and his French comrades, specially drawn up in my candle-lit command post in the underground tunnel. In my French address, I said that the bearing of this young volunteer was what we had come to expect of French soldiers, men who had won their spurs on the battlefields throughout the world. On the same day, the commander of 503 Panzer Section, Major Herzig, was decorated with the Knight's Cross by Major-General Mohnke. These were the last two such decorations awarded.'

By 30 April what remained of the Nordland and the Charlemagne Divisions had been driven back to within 1,000 yards of the Reichskanzlei. There, in the Führerbunker, Hitler at long last realised that the end was near, married his mistress Eva Braun, and committed suicide. The news of his death 'fighting to save Germany from Bolshevism'

reached the SS survivors on 1 May. It was the moment of truth for them and the one thought uppermost in their minds was to fall into American rather than Soviet hands. That night, under cover of darkness, some of them tried to fight their way through the Russian ring encircling the capital. Only a few got through; the rest were killed or captured. SS-Brigadeführer Siegler, who had escaped from the Führerbunker, was also killed.

Berlin surrendered that night; the war was finished and with it the Waffen-SS.

146
Victory Parade in Red Square Moscow. Captured standards and Colours of German units and formations were thrown at Stalin's feet.

146

Appendices

1 Comparative Ranks

The table which follows sets out the ranks of the SS and the corresponding ranks in the German, British and American armies and the German police. Rank titles of senior SS officers were often dual owing to the amalgamation of the police with the SS and to the creation of the Waffen SS. Thus an SS general who was also a police general was, eg an SS-Gruppenführer and Generalleutnant der Polizei, or if he was seconded to, or promoted within, the Waffen-SS he was, eg an SS-Brigadeführer and Generalmajor der Waffen-SS.

Note: This table is a representative comparison of ranks not an actual comparison

SS	German Army	British Army	US Army	German Police
No equivalent	Generalfeldmarschall	Field Marshal	General of the Army	
Oberstgruppenführer	Generaloberst	General	General	Generaloberst der Polizei
Obergruppenführer	General (der Infanterie etc)	Lieutenant-General	Lieutenant-General	General der Polizei
Gruppenführer	Generalleutnant	Major-General	Major-General	Generalleutnant der Polizei
Brigadeführer	Generalmajor	Brigadier	Brigadier-General	Generalmajor der Polizei
Oberführer	No equivalent	No equivalent	No equivalent	Oberst der Schutzpolizei or Gendarmerie
Standartenführer	Oberst	Colonel	Colonel	Reichskriminaldirektor
Obersturmbannführer	Oberstleutnant	Lieutenant-Colonel	Lieutenant-Colonel	Oberstleutnant der Schupo or Gendarmerie Oberregierungs und Kriminalrat
Sturmbannführer	Major	Major	Major	Major der Schutzpolizei or Gendarmerie Regierungs- und Kriminalrat Kriminaldirektor
Hauptsturmführer	Hauptmann	Captain	Captain	Hauptmann der Schutzpolizei or Gendarmerie, Kriminalrat
Obersturmführer	Oberleutnant	Lieutenant	First Lieutenant	Oberleutnant der Schutzpolizei or Gendarmerie Kriminalkommissar Kriminalinspektor
Untersturmführer	Leutnant	Second Lieutenant	Second Lieutenant	Leutnant der Schutzpolizei or Gendarmerie Kriminalsekretär Kriminaloberassistent
Sturmscharführer	Stabsfeldwebel Stabswachtmeister	WO 1	Chief WO	Meister Kriminalsekretär
Stabsscharführer	Hauptfeldwebel	Quartermaster Sergeant-Major	WO	Hauptwachtmeister
Hauptscharführer	Hauptwachtmeister			Kriminaloberassistent Kompaniehauptwachtmeister
Oberscharführer	Oberfeldwebel	Staff Sergeant	Master Sergeant	Revieroberwachtmeister Kriminalassistent Oberwachtmeister Kriminalassistent

SS	German Army	British Army	US Army	German Police
Scharführer	Feldwebel	Sergeant	Sergeant	Wachtmeister Kriminalassistentanwärter
Unterscharführer	Unterfeldwebel	No equivalent	No equivalent	Unterwachtmeister
No equivalent	Unteroffizier	No equivalent	No equivalent	No equivalent
Rottenführer Sturmmann SS-Obersaut	Stabsgefreiter Gefreiter	Corporal Lance Corporal	Corporal No equivalent	No equivalent No equivalent
SS-Oberschütze	Oberschütze Obergrenadier etc	No equivalent	Private First Class	No equivalent
SS-Mann	Schütze	Private	Private	Anwärter

2 SS Divisions 1940–5

No	Type	Name	Remarks
1	SS Panzer Division	Leibstandarte Adolf Hitler	Formed from bodyguard troops
2	SS Panzer Division	Das Reich	Original Verfügungs Div
3	SS Panzer Division	Totenkopf	
4	SS Panzergrenadier Division	Polizei	
5*	SS Panzer Division	Wiking	
6	SS Gebirgsdivision	Nord	From Totenkopf troops
7†	SS Freiwillige Gebirgsdivision	Prinz Eugen	
8	SS Kavallerie Division	Florian Geyer	
9	SS Panzer Division	Hohenstaufen	
10	SS Panzer Division	Frundsberg	
11*	SS Freiwillige Panzergrenadier Division	Nordland	Partly from National legions
12	SS Panzer Division	Hitlerjugend	Mainly from members of Nazi Youth Movement
13*	Waffen Gebirgsdivision der SS	Handschar	
14*	Waffen-Grenadier Division der SS	(Galiz No 1)	
15*	Waffen-Grenadier Division der SS	(Lett No 1)	
16†	SS Panzergrenadier	Reichsführer SS	
17†	SS Panzergrenadier	Götz von Berlichingen	
18†	SS Panzergrenadier (freiwillige)	Horst Wessel	

No	Type	Name	Remarks
19*	Waffen-Grenadier Division der SS	(Lett No 2)	
20*	Waffen-Grenadier Division der SS	(Estn No 2)	
21*‡	Waffen Gebirgsdivision der SS	Skanderberg	Mainly Albanian troops
22*	Freiwillige Kavallerie Division der SS	Maria Theresia	
23*‡	Waffen-Grenadier Division der SS	Kama (Croat)	Designation used for PG Division Nederland 1944
24‡	Waffen Gebirgskarstjäger Division der SS	—	Reputed of low quality Alpine troops
25*‡	Waffen-Grenadier Division	Hunyadi	(Ungar No 1)
26*‡	Waffen-Grenadier Division	(Ungar No 2)	Both of Hungarian origin
27*‡	SS Freiwillige-Grenadier Division	Langemarck	
28*‡	SS Freiwillige-Grenadier Division	Wallonien	
29*	SS Freiwillige-Grenadier Division	(Russ No 1)	Number given to Italian SS in 1945
30*	SS Freiwillige-Grenadier Division	(Russ No 2)	
31*‡	SS Freiwillige Panzergrenadier Division	Böhmen-Mähren	Established 1945 by School troops in Czechoslovakia
32*	SS Panzergrenadier	30 Januar	Formed 1945 from training troops
33*‡	Waffen Kavallerie Division der SS	(Ungar No 3)	Annihilated 1945 and number given to SS Charlemagne
34*‡	SS Freiwillige-Grenadier Division	Landstorm Nederland	
35*‡	SS Polizei-Grenadier Division	—	Formed 1945
36*	Waffen-Grenadier Division	—	Dirlewanger Brigade upgraded
37*‡	SS Freiwillige Kavallerie Division	Lützow	
38‡	SS Panzergrenadier	Nibelungen	Formed 1945 partly from staff of officers school at Bad Tölz

Notes:

* Partly or mainly from foreign troops.

† Partly or mainly from Volksdeutsche.

‡ These formations were never more than of regimental strength.

There were also several nominally battalion or regiment sized units including the two embryo Cossack Divisions and all made up of foreign troops except the crack *Begleit Battalion* (mot) *Reichsführer SS* and the *Wachtbattalion* (mot), *Leibstandarte Adolf Hitler*, which were bodyguard units.

Note: The *Handschar* Division was an odd ephemeral unit whose name was used as a cover for movement of other Divisions.

3 Organisation of Divisions

For the purpose of this appendix the organisation shown is based on that of the Leibstandarte Adolf Hitler Division. Other Waffen-SS divisions were similarly organised but individual establishments varied according to the type it was operating and quality of the division itself (ie as may be expected the non-Germanic divisions were on a lower establishment as regards both men and equipment).

In September 1939 the Leibstandarte had a combat strength of 3,700 men, organised into four infantry battalions and supporting units comprising a mortar company, an infantry gun company, an anti-tank company, a motorcycle company and an engineer platoon. By May 1940 it had gained one more infantry-gun company, a light-infantry column and an artillery battalion of three batteries of 10.5cm field guns. In August 1940 Hitler authorised the further expansion of the Leibstandarte to brigade strength and an artillery regiment, an engineer battalion, a signals company and a reconnaissance detachment were raised. Thus, at the end of the reorganisation of the Leibstandarte before the Balkan campaign, its composition was as follows:

Headquarters staff
Three battalions, each of three rifle, one machine gun and one heavy company (the heavy company consisting of two anti-tank gun platoons (3.7cm and 5cm Pak) and one each of mortars (8cm) and pioneers).

A fourth, heavy battalion of one light infantry gun company (7.5cm), one heavy infantry gun company (15cm), one anti-tank gun company (4.7cm self-propelled), one field-gun company (7.5cm self-propelled) and one anti-aircraft gun company (3.7cm). A fifth, guard battalion of four companies (then stationed at Berlin-Lichterfelde). A reconnaissance detachment with two motorcycle companies, one armoured car company (Sd Kfz 222 and Sd Kfz 233) and one heavy company.

An artillery regiment, with one battalion of three batteries (10.5cm), one mixed battalion of three batteries (two of 15cm and one of 8.8cm guns) and one light artillery column.

An engineer battalion with three companies, a bridging column and a light engineer column.

A signals detachment with one telephone and one wireless company.
Miscellaneous supply and service units.

Before the start of the Russian campaign the Leibstandarte was strengthened by the addition of another infantry battalion, an anti-aircraft detachment of three batteries (two of 3.7cm and one of 2cm Flak), a survey battery, a light signals column, and a field hospital. Its strength on 30 June 1941 was 10,796 men.

Expansion continued, and on 9 September 1942 Hitler decreed that his Guard should be known as the SS Panzergrenadier Division Leibstandarte Adolf Hitler. Two panzergrenadier regiments had been formed out of the existing infantry battalions in mid-1942, and an assault-gun detachment (Sturmgeschütz III) and a self-propelled anti-tank gun detachment (7.5cm Pak 'Marder') had been created.

In October 1942, the composition of an SS panzergrenadier regiment was given as:

Headquarters and band.
Escort company: motorcycle despatch platoon and signals platoon.
Three battalions, each of three companies (of three platoons), one machine gun company, and one heavy company, consisting of one anti-tank (5cm), one light infantry gun and one engineer platoon.
One heavy infantry gun company (self-propelled) (15cm Bison).
One anti-tank company (self-propelled) (7.5cm).
One anti-aircraft company (self-propelled) (2cm).

Of more significance for the future however was the establishment of a tank battalion (Abteilung) of three companies in January 1942; this was equipped with Panzer IIIs and IVs. In October and November of the same year a tank regiment was formed out of this nucleus — SS Panzer Regiment 1 (two battalions). In December the Leibstandarte received two companies with the new Tigers (22 tanks). In the first half of 1943, 100 Panthers arrived and the tank regiment was organised as follows (a paper strength of some 250 tanks):

Headquarters

Three battalions each of four companies and a heavy company and an Engineer Company.

In the autumn of 1943, when the Division moved to Italy, the regiment lost its third battalion.

On 31 December 1942 the strength of the Leibstandarte was 678 officers and 20,166 other ranks (considerably higher than Army divisions), and by the end of 1943 a total of 19,867. On 22 October 1943 the unit received its final title — I SS Panzer Division Leibstandarte Adolf Hitler (it had been a full armoured division in all but name for over a year).

Hitler's Guard was now of such a size that it took nearly 150 trains to move the Division minus its armour from the East to Italy.

In March 1944 the Order of Battle of the Leibstandarte was as follows:

Divisional headquarters

SS Panzer-Grenadier Regiment No 1
Headquarters
I Battalion with 1-5 Companies
II Battalion with 6-10 Companies
III Battalion with 11-15 Companies
16 Anti-aircraft Company
17 Infantry-gun Company
18 Anti-tank Company
19 Reconnaissance Company
20 Engineer Company

SS Panzer-Grenadier Regiment No 2
Headquarters
I Battalion with 1-5 Companies
II Battalion with 6-10 Companies
III Battalion with 11-14 Companies
15 Anti-aircraft Company
16 Infantry-gun Company
17 Anti-tank Company
18 Reconnaissance Company
19 Engineer Company

SS Panzer-Reconnaissance Detachment No 1
Headquarters
1-6 Companies

SS Panzer Regiment No 1
Headquarters
I Battalion with 1-4 Companies
II Battalion with 5-8 Companies
Heavy Company
Engineer Company

SS Panzer Anti-Tank Detachment No 1
Headquarters
1-3 Companies

SS Assault Gun Detachment No 1
Headquarters
1-3 Companies

SS Panzer Artillery Regiment No 1
Headquarters
I Battalion with 1-3 Batteries
II Battalion with 4-6 Batteries
III Battalion with 7-9 Batteries
IV Battalion with 10-12 Batteries

SS Anti-Aircraft Detachment No 1
Headquarters
1-5 Companies
2cm Flak Platoon

SS Panzer Pioneer Battalion No 1
Headquarters
1-4 Companies

SS Panzer Signals Detachment No 1
Headquarters
1-2 Companies

On 1 June 1944 the Leibstandarte consisted of 21,386 men, armed with 45 self-propelled guns and 50 Panzer IV, 38 Panther, and 29 Tiger tanks.
In September 1944 the following unit was added:

SS Mortar Detachment No 1
Headquarters
1-3 Batteries (15cm)
4 Battery (21cm)

A return of strengths on 20 September gave nominal numbers of 655 officers, 4,177 NCOs, 14,246 men and 1,029 helpers (20,107).

By mid-December the Leibstandarte had within its battle order 84 tanks and 20 self-propelled guns with the promise of more to come.

For the Ardennes Offensive the Leibstandarte formed Kampfgruppe Peiper which consisted of:

I Battalion Panzer Regiment
III Battalion Panzer Grenadier Regiment No 2
II Battalion Artillery Regiment
3 Company Pioneer Battalion

Reconnaissance Detachment
68 Flak Battalion (Luftwaffe)
501 Heavy Panzer Battalion (I SS Panzer Corps) (Tiger IIs).

The I Panzer Battalion was a mixture of the strongest companies of the Regiment, viz:

Headquarters
1 Company (Mk V) ⎫
2 Company (Mk V) ⎭ 60 tanks
6 Company (Mk VI) ⎫
7 Company (Mk VI) ⎭ 60 tanks
9 Company (Engineers)
Artillery

The Leibstandarte's last battle took enormous toll of its strength at a time when no adequate reinforcements were forthcoming. The situation was so bad that on 7 April 1945 Hitler's Guard was down to a mere 57 officers, 229 NCOs, 1,296 men and 16 tanks in the field.

Just as Hitler ensured that his Guard received large numbers of personnel, so he saw to it that it received generous quantities of the latest and best equipment.

4 Foreign Nationals Serving in the SS Division Wiking

On its formation the Wiking Division consisted of the German SS Regiment Germania, and two regiments of foreigners — Nordland and Westland. Nordland was manned by Norwegians and Danes, Westland by Dutchmen and Flemings (from Belgium). As the war progressed volunteers from other so-called Germanic countries enlisted in the division and the following list details those countries.

Britain

About a dozen British renegades volunteered for service with the Wiking. It is doubtful if any of them saw a shot fired in anger, and when the war ended they were apprehended in northern Germany.

Denmark

Most of the Danes served in the Nordland Regiment which, at its formation, was approximately 40% Danish. There were never less than about one thousand Danes serving with the Wiking and in September 1944 there were about 1,400 officers and other ranks.

Finland

In 1941 the division included a Finnish contingent of about 400.

Flanders (Flemish-speaking Belgium)

A few Flemings served with the division — mainly in the Westland Regiment.

France

A French volunteer battalion (*französisches Freiwilligen Bataillon*) commanded by SS-Hauptsturmführer Henri Joseph Feret, attached to the division fought in Russia and ended up in Berlin in 1945. The SS-Sturmbrigade Wallonien was formed from inhabitants of French-speaking Belgium.

Germany

Most of the staff and supporting arms as well as something like 25% of the fighting strength of the division were German nationals. Replacements for casualties were often ethnic Germans (Volksdeutsche) from countries such as Hungary, Rumania, Latvia, Estonia etc.

Netherlands

Most of the Dutch contingent (approximately 600 volunteers in 1941) served in the Westland Regiment.

Norway

The majority of the Norwegians with Wiking (about 300 volunteers initially) were concentrated in the Nordland Regiment.

Sweden

A handful of Swedes did serve with the division but the volunteer Swedish legion never materialised (only one volunteer was forthcoming when the idea was mooted in 1941).

Switzerland

Some Swiss are reputed to have served with the Wiking, mainly with the artillery.

147

148

126

147
A group of Moslem volunteers from the 13th SS Division Handschar. The 'Mujos' as they were called by the Germans were maltreated by their German superiors and in September 1943 1,000 of them mutinied and killed a number of their officers and NCOs. The Moslem chaplains, the Imams, of which there was one with every battalion, helped to cool the situation and the Grand Mufti of Jerusalem who was living in Berlin visited the division to help restore order.

148
The Grand Mufti of Jerusalem inspects 'Mujos' of the Handschar Division. While fighting the partisans in Yugoslavia the men of this division are said to have followed the example of their SS colleagues of the Prinz Eugen Division in committing atrocities. (Imperial War Museum)

150

149
A military policeman of the Handschar Division (a German) checks the identity of a Moslem woman.

150
SS mountain troops of the 6th SS-Gebirgs Division Nord undergoing training.

151
SS-Standartenführer
Deisenhofer, 17 July 1944.